Famous Biographies for Young People

Books by Roland J. McKinney

DEGAS

THE EIGHT

THOMAS EAKINS

FAMOUS OLD MASTERS OF PAINTING

FAMOUS AMERICAN PAINTERS

Famous American Painters

by Roland J. McKinney

ILLUSTRATED WITH REPRODUCTIONS
OF THE ARTISTS' PAINTINGS

Dodd, Mead & Company

NEW YORK

To my sons Roland and Peter

Contents

List of Painters and Location of Their Work*

JOHN SMYBERT
Boston, Mass. (Museum); Cambridge, Mass. (Fogg Art Museum); Cleveland, Ohio (Museum); Hartford, Conn. (Wadsworth, Atheneum); New Haven, Conn. (Yale University Gallery of Fine Arts); New York, N.Y. (Metropolitan Museum); Salem, Mass. (Essex Institute); Worcester, Mass. (Museum).

JOHN SINGLETON COPLEY
Boston, Mass. (Museum); Cambridge, Mass. (Fogg Art Museum); Chicago, Ill. (Art Institute); Cleveland, Ohio (Museum); Detroit, Mich. (Institute of Arts); Hartford, Conn. (Wadsworth Atheneum); Kansas City, Mo. (William Rockhill Nelson Gallery); New York, N.Y. (Metropolitan Museum, Public Library); Philadelphia, Pa. (Historical Society of Pennsylvania); Salem, Mass. (Essex Institute); Washington, D.C. (National Gallery).

GILBERT STUART
Baltimore, Md. (Museum); Boston, Mass. (Atheneum, Museum); Chicago, Ill. (Art Institute); Cincinnati, Ohio (Museum); Cleveland, Ohio (Museum); Detroit, Mich. (Institute of Arts); Fort Worth, Texas (Art Association); Hartford, Conn. (Wadsworth Atheneum); Minneapolis, Minn. (Institute of Arts); New York, N.Y. (Historical Society, Metropolitan Museum, Museum of the City of New York); Philadelphia, Pa. (Pennsylvania Academy of Fine Arts, Museum); Pittsburgh, Pa. (Carnegie Institute); Pittsfield, Mass. (Berkshire Museum); Providence, R.I. (Rhode Island School of Design); Salem, Mass. (Essex Institute); Toledo, Ohio (Museum); Washington, D.C. (Corcoran Gallery, National Gallery); Worcester, Mass. (Museum).

GEORGE INNESS
Andover, Mass. (Addison Gallery); Baltimore, Md. (Peabody Institute); Bloomfield Hills, Mich. (Cranbrook Academy of Art); Boston, Mass. (Museum); Brunswick, Me. (Bowdoin College Museum of Fine Arts); Buffalo, N.Y. (Albright Art Gallery); Cambridge, Mass. (Fogg Art Museum); Chicago, Ill. (Art Institute); Cincinnati, Ohio (Museum); Cleveland, Ohio (Museum); Davenport, Iowa (Municipal Art Gallery); Detroit, Mich. (Institute of Arts); Fort Worth, Texas (Art Association); Hartford, Conn. (Wadsworth Atheneum); Houston, Texas (Museum); Indianapolis, Ind. (John Herron Art Institute); Lawrence, Kansas (Thayer Museum of Art); Kansas City, Mo. (William Rockhill Nelson

* This information is not complete, as new acquisitions are constantly being made by art institutions.

7

LIST OF PAINTERS

Gallery); Manchester, N.H. (Currier Gallery of Art); Milwaukee, Wisc. (Layton Art Gallery); Minneapolis, Minn. (Walker Art Gallery); Montclair, N.J. (Museum); New York, N.Y. (Brooklyn Museum, Historical Society, Metropolitan Museum); Northampton, Mass. (Smith College Museum of Art); Philadelphia, Pa. (Museum); Pittsburgh, Pa. (Carnegie Institute); Pittsfield, Mass. (Berkshire Museum); Princeton, N.J. (Museum of Historic Art); Providence, R.I. (Rhode Island School of Design); San Francisco, Cal. (California Palace of the Legion of Honor); Seattle, Wash. (University of Washington, Henry Art Gallery); Toledo, Ohio (Museum); Washington, D.C. (Corcoran Gallery, National Gallery, Phillips Memorial Gallery); Worcester, Mass. (Museum).

JAMES McNEILL WHISTLER

Andover, Mass. (Addison Gallery); Boston, Mass. (Isabella Stewart Gardner Museum, Museum); Cambridge, Mass. (Fogg Art Museum); Chicago, Ill. (Art Institute); Cincinnati, Ohio (Museum); Cleveland, Ohio (Museum); Columbus, Ohio (Gallery of Fine Arts); Detroit, Mich. (Institute of Arts); Haverford, Pa. (Haverford College Museum of Fine Arts); Kansas City, Mo. (William Rockhill Nelson Gallery); Muskegon, Mich. (Hackley Art Gallery); New Haven, Conn. (Yale University Art Gallery); New York, N.Y. (Brooklyn Museum, Frick Art Gallery, Metropolitan Museum); Northampton, Mass. (Smith College Art Museum); Philadelphia, Pa. (Museum); Pittsburgh, Pa. (Carnegie Institute); Providence, R.I. (Rhode Island School of Design); Syracuse, N.Y. (Museum); Toledo, Ohio (Museum); Washington, D.C. (Freer Gallery of Art, including the Peacock Room, National Gallery, Phillips Memorial Gallery); Worcester, Mass. (Museum).

WINSLOW HOMER

Andover, Mass. (Addison Gallery); Baltimore, Md. (Peabody Institute); Boston, Mass. (Museum); Brunswick, Me. (Bowdoin College Museum of Fine Arts); Cambridge, Mass. (Fogg Art Museum); Canajoharie, N.Y. (Public Library and Art Gallery); Chicago, Ill. (Art Institute); Cincinnati, Ohio (Museum); Cleveland, Ohio (Museum); Denver, Col. (Museum); Detroit, Mich. (Institute of Arts); Hartford, Conn. (Wadsworth Atheneum); Haverford, Pa. (Haverford College Art Museum); Indianapolis, Indiana (John Herron Art Institute); Laurel, Miss. (Lauren Rogers Library and Museum); Lawrence, Kan. (Thayer Museum of Art);

8

LIST OF PAINTERS

Los Angeles, Cal. (County Museum); Manchester, N.H. (Currier Gallery of Art); Milwaukee, Wisc. (Layton Art Gallery); Minneapolis, Minn. (Institute of Arts); New York, N.Y. (Brooklyn Museum, Cooper Union, Metropolitan Museum, Whitney Museum); Northampton, Mass. (Smith College Art Museum); Philadelphia, Pa. (Pennsylvania Academy of Fine Arts, Museum); Pittsburgh, Pa. (Carnegie Institute); Princeton, N.J. (Museum of Historic Art); Providence, R.I. (Rhode Island School of Design); Washington, D.C. (Corcoran Gallery, Freer Gallery of Art, National Gallery, Phillips Memorial Gallery); Worcester, Mass. (Museum).

THOMAS EAKINS

Andover, Mass. (Addison Gallery); Boston, Mass. (Museum); Chicago, Ill. (Art Institute); Cleveland, Ohio (Museum); Detroit, Mich. (Institute of Arts); Fort Worth, Texas (Art Association); Marion, Pa. (Barnes Foundation); New Haven, Conn. (Yale University Art Gallery); New York, N.Y. (Brooklyn Museum, Metropolitan Museum, National Academy of Design, Whitney Museum); Northampton, Mass. (Smith College Museum of Art); Philadelphia, Pa. (Jefferson Medical College, Pennsylvania Academy of Fine Arts, Museum, University of Pennsylvania); Pittsburgh, Pa. (Carnegie Institute); Washington, D.C. (Catholic University, Corcoran Gallery, National Gallery, Phillips Memorial Gallery); Wichita, Kan. (Museum).

MARY CASSATT

Andover, Mass. (Addison Gallery); Baltimore, Md. (Museum, Peabody Institute, Walters Art Gallery); Boston, Mass. (Museum); Cambridge, Mass. (Fogg Art Museum); Chicago, Ill. (Art Institute); Cincinnati, Ohio (Museum); Cleveland, Ohio (Museum); Detroit, Mich. (Institute of Arts); Hartford, Conn. (Wadsworth Atheneum); Indianapolis, Ind. (John Herron Art Institute); Los Angeles, Cal. (County Museum); Newark, N.J. (Museum); New Haven, Conn. (Yale University Art Gallery); New York, N.Y. (Metropolitan Museum); Omaha, Neb. (Joslyn Memorial Art Museum); Philadelphia, Pa. (Museum); Pittsburgh, Pa. (Carnegie Institute); Providence, R.I. (Rhode Island School of Design); Washington, D.C. (Corcoran Gallery, National Gallery); Wichita, Kan. (Museum).

ALBERT PINKHAM RYDER

Akron, Ohio (Art Institute); Amherst, Mass. (Amherst College Museum); Andover, Mass. (Addison Gallery); Athens, Geor-

9

LIST OF PAINTERS

gia (University of Georgia Museum); Boston, Mass. (Museum); Buffalo, N.Y. (Albright Art Gallery); Cambridge, Mass. (Fogg Art Museum); Chicago, Ill. (Art Institute); Cleveland, Ohio (Museum); Columbus, Ohio (Gallery of Fine Arts); Detroit, Mich. (Institute of Arts); Haverford, Pa. (Haverford College Art Museum); Lynchburg, Va. (Randolph-Macon Woman's College); Minneapolis, Minn. (Institute of Arts, Walker Art Center); New York, N.Y. (Brooklyn Museum, Metropolitan Museum, Whitney Museum); Northampton, Mass. (Smith College Museum of Art); Rochester, N.Y. (Memorial Art Gallery); St. Louis, Mo. (City Art Museum); Toledo, Ohio (Museum); San Diego, Cal. (Fine Arts Society); Washington, D.C. (Freer Gallery of Art, National Gallery, Phillips Memorial Gallery); Wichita, Kan. (Museum); Worcester, Mass. (Museum); Youngstown, Ohio (Butler Art Institute).

JOHN SINGER SARGENT

Andover, Mass. (Addison Gallery); Baltimore, Md. (Johns Hopkins University, Welch Library); Boston, Mass. (Museum, Public Library); Buffalo, N.Y. (Albright Art Gallery); Cambridge, Mass. (Fogg Art Museum, Widener Library); Chicago, Ill. (Art Institute); Cincinnati, Ohio (Taft Museum); Cleveland, Ohio (Museum); Columbus, Ohio (Gallery of Fine Arts); Detroit, Mich. (Institute of Arts); Hartford, Conn. (Wadsworth Atheneum); Indianapolis, Ind. (John Herron Art Institute); Los Angeles, Cal. (County Museum); Minneapolis, Minn. (Institute of Arts); New York, N.Y. (Brooklyn Museum, Metropolitan Museum); Northampton, Mass. (Smith College Museum of Art); Philadelphia, Pa. (Pennsylvania Academy of Fine Arts, Museum); Providence, R.I. (Rhode Island School of Design); Toledo, Ohio (Museum); Washington, D.C. (Corcoran Gallery, Freer Gallery of Art, National Gallery).

MAURICE PRENDERGAST

Andover, Mass. (Addison Gallery); Boston, Mass. (Museum); Cambridge, Mass. (Fogg Art Museum); Chicago, Ill. (Art Institute); Cleveland, Ohio (Museum); Columbus, Ohio (Gallery of Fine Arts); Detroit, Mich. (Institute of Arts); Los Angeles, Cal. (County Museum); Marion, Pa. (Barnes Foundation); Newark, N.J. (Museum); New Britain, Conn. (Museum of the New Britain Institute); New Haven, Conn. (Yale University Art Gallery); New York, N.Y. (Metropolitan Museum, Museum of Modern Art, Whitney Museum); Washington, D.C. (Phillips Memorial Gallery).

10

LIST OF PAINTERS

ROBERT HENRI

Andover, Mass. (Addison Gallery); Boston, Mass. (Museum); Buffalo, N.Y. (Albright Art Gallery); Chicago, Ill. (Art Institute); Cincinnati, Ohio (Museum); Columbus, Ohio (Gallery of Fine Arts); Dallas, Texas (Museum); Decatur, Ill. (Art Center); Des Moines, Iowa (Art Center); Detroit, Mich. (Institute of Arts); Kansas City, Mo. (Art Institute); Lawrence, Kan. (Thayer Museum of Art); Los Angeles, Cal. (County Museum); Memphis, Tenn. (Brooks Memorial Art Gallery); Milwaukee, Wisc. (Art Institute); Montclair, N.J. (Museum); Newark, N.J. (Museum); New Haven, Conn. (Yale University Art Gallery); New Orleans, La. (Isaac Delgado Museum of Art); New York, N.Y. (Brooklyn Museum, Metropolitan Museum, National Arts Club, Whitney Museum); Oberlin, Ohio (Dudley Peter Allen Memorial Museum); Philadelphia, Pa. (Pennsylvania Academy of Fine Arts); Pittsburgh, Pa. (Carnegie Institute); Providence, R.I. (Rhode Island School of Design); Rochester, N.Y. (Memorial Art Gallery); St. Louis, Mo. (City Art Museum); San Diego, Cal. (Fine Arts Society); San Francisco, Cal. (Museum); Santa Fe, N.M. (Museum of New Mexico); Savannah, Ga. (Telfair Academy of Arts and Sciences); Toledo, Ohio (Museum); Washington, D.C. (Corcoran Gallery, National Gallery, Phillips Memorial Gallery); Wichita, Kan. (Museum); Wilmington, Del. (Society of the Fine Arts); Youngstown, Ohio (Butler Art Institute).

GEORGE BELLOWS

Andover, Mass. (Addison Gallery); Baltimore, Md. (Peabody Institute); Boston, Mass. (Museum); Buffalo, N.Y. (Albright Art Gallery); Cambridge, Mass. (Fogg Art Museum); Chicago, Ill. (Art Institute); Cincinnati, Ohio (Institute of Arts); Cleveland, Ohio (Museum); Columbus, Ohio (Gallery of Fine Arts); Des Moines, Iowa (Art Center); Detroit, Mich. (Institute of Arts); Los Angeles, Cal. (County Museum); Minneapolis, Minn. (Institute of Arts); Newark, N.J. (Museum); New Britain, Conn. (Art Museum of the New Britain Institute); New York, N.Y. (Brooklyn Museum, Metropolitan Museum, Whitney Museum); Philadelphia, Pa. (Pennsylvania Academy of Fine Arts); Pittsburgh, Pa. (Carnegie Institute); Providence, R.I. (Rhode Island School of Design); San Diego, Cal. (Fine Arts Society); Savannah, Ga. (Telfair Academy of Arts and Sciences); Toledo, Ohio (Museum); Washington, D.C. (Corcoran Gallery, National Gallery, Phillips Memorial Gallery); Worcester, Mass. (Museum).

Illustrations

(See Supplement which follows)

JOHN SMYBERT THE BERMUDA GROUP
Courtesy of Yale University Art Gallery

JOHN SINGLETON COPLEY PORTRAIT OF PAUL REVERE
Courtesy Museum of Fine Arts, Boston

GILBERT STUART MRS. RICHARD YATES
Courtesy of the National Gallery of Art, Washing-
ton, D. C. (Mellon Collection)

GEORGE INNESS MOONLIGHT ON PASSAMAQUODDY BAY
Courtesy of the Art Institute of Chicago

JAMES MCNEILL WHISTLER THE WHITE GIRL
Courtesy of the National Gallery of Art, Washing-
ton, D. C. (Harris Whittemore Collection)

WINSLOW HOMER THE HERRING NET
Courtesy of the Art Institute of Chicago

THOMAS EAKINS SIGNORA GOMEZ D'ARZA
Courtesy of The Metropolitan Museum of Art

ILLUSTRATIONS

Illustrative Supplement

JOHN SMYBERT: —*The Bermuda Group*

JOHN SINGLETON COPLEY:—*Portrait of Paul Revere*

GILBERT STUART:—*Mrs. Richard Yates*

GEORGE INNESS:—*Moonlight on Passamaquoddy Bay*

James McNeill Whistler:—*The White Girl*

WINSLOW HOMER:—*The Herring Net*

THOMAS EAKINS:—*Signora Gomez D'Arza*

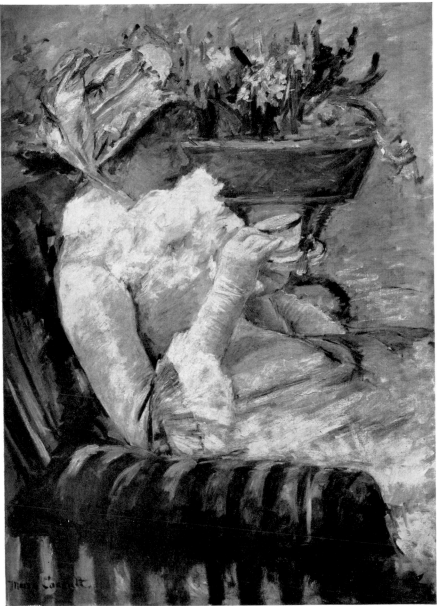

MARY CASSATT:—*The Cup of Tea*

ALBERT PINKHAM RYDER:—*Toilers of the Sea*

JOHN SINGER SARGENT:—*Robert Louis Stevenson*

MAURICE PRENDERGAST:—*Beachmont*

ROBERT HENRI:—*Sea and Cliffs*

GEORGE BELLOWS:—*Lady Jean*

John Smybert
1684?-1751

John Smybert
1684?-1751

"WESTWARD the course of Empire takes its way" is a familiar phrase to most Americans, but few realize that these words were written by a man who, in his enthusiasm to establish cultural standards in the New World, induced a successful painter in London, at the age of forty-four, to seek his fortune anew in America. The writer of this stanza, which appears in the prophetic poem, *America*, was Dean George Berkeley, of Derry, the noted Irish clergyman and philosopher; the artist was John Smybert, born in 1684, in Edinburgh, Scotland.

These two men set sail in the autumn of 1728 from Gravesend, England, bound for Bermuda, where Dean Berkeley hoped to found a mission school. The voyagers landed four months later at Newport, Rhode Island, instead. This was the result of trusting themselves to a ship's captain who failed to understand the vagaries of wind and current, a common occurrence in those early days of navigation. During the long voyage, Smybert made drawings of the Dean and his companions for use in a large painting he was planning to make of the Berkeley party.

Soon after landing, the Dean purchased a farm at Newport, where he settled down with his friends to await the King's final approval of the Bermuda project. Here Smybert completed work on the painting he had begun aboard ship.

Now known as, *Dean Berkeley and His Entourage,* the picture is believed to be the first large group painting done in America.

Represented in the picture, besides the Dean standing to the right of the table, is his secretary, seated at the opposite end, taking dictation. Also, Miss Handcock and Mrs. Berkeley, with an infant in her arms, are seated near the Dean, while Mr. James and John Moffat stand behind the ladies. Smybert included his own portrait in the upper left of the picture. Through the columns in the background may be seen a view of Narragansett Bay. Dean Berkeley remained in Newport about two years, waiting for the promised funds for his mission school. However, support by the Crown was withdrawn and the Dean was forced to abandon his cherished dream.

Before he returned to Ireland, Berkeley presented Yale University with a library of one thousand volumes, and, in addition, he gave his Newport farm to the University, with the stipulation that any income derived from it should be used for scholarships to be awarded to worthy and capable students in the classics.

Meanwhile, Smybert had left for Boston to try to establish himself as a painter. He must have been impressed when he looked upon the city for the first time. There were many finely designed churches and rows of well-built houses. Quite a few of the streets were paved with stone blocks down the middle. These were used by pedestrians as well as vehicles, since no sidewalks existed in the town. Numerous craft shops flourished where young native apprentices (Paul Revere and Benjamin Franklin among them) were bound to a long period of study in a chosen craft, such as silver-making, printing, or furniture construction, under the guidance of artisans who had worked at their professions in the Old World and were re-establishing themselves in the Bay Colony.

There were other shops where ladies and gentlemen could find the latest fashions from London, quaintly advertised in the newspapers as, "Bonnets proper for Widows and other Ladies, made in the genteelest manner" . . . "neat silk shoes" . . . "Pink colored short Aprons and Stomachers for Young Ladies" . . . "A very fine Assortment of Men's plain mixt, motled, diced and peck'd Stockings, all very good" . . . "Wiggs" . . . "20 suits London-made Claret & other Colored Cloth Coats, Vests & Breeches" . . . "new fashion thread blond lace for Gentlemen's Ruffles . . ."

Commerce flowed into the city through Long Wharf, which extended nearly half a mile into the Bay. The north side of the pier was lined with shipping offices, taverns, and stores; the south side was dredged deep to permit the largest ocean going vessels to dock.

Trade between England and the colony was confined mostly to imports, under an edict of the Crown, but the colonists, needing the give and take of foreign trade to prosper, developed their own markets with the West Indies which were outside Britain's control. Boston, through the courage and vision of its leaders, soon became the metropolis of the colonies.

Smybert was the first qualified painter to settle in America up to that time; but he was aware that he could not depend on portrait work alone to assure his support. He accordingly opened a shop on Cornhill, not far from Dock Square, where he announced in the newspapers that he offered for sale, ". . . all sorts of Colors, dry and ground, with Oils & Brushes, Frames of several sorts, the best Metzotints, Italian, French, Dutch & English prints in Frames & Glasses or without, by Wholesale or Retail." His painting rooms were located in the shop, their walls lined with copies of paintings by the Old Masters which he had carefully executed during his student days in Rome. These were a source of wonder to his students and patrons, as they were the only likenesses of famous paintings then to be seen in Boston.

Among the noted people who visited Smybert's rooms to be painted was Peter Faneuil, wealthy Boston merchant and patriot, who also engaged the artist to design a combination market place and meeting hall which Faneuil wished to give to the city. In 1742, Smybert drew up plans for a two-story building, arched and open on the street level, where farmers could display their produce, while the second floor was designed for town meetings. The building, enlarged in 1762 after a disastrous fire, became known as Faneuil Hall, "Cradle of Liberty," as it was here that patriotic meetings were held by the citizens of Boston in protest against British rule.

Smybert married Mary Williams, the daughter of Nathaniel Williams, Jr. Two children were born of the marriage. Between shopkeeping, teaching art, and painting portraits and "landskips," Smybert achieved a certain prosperity.

He purchased property in Boston and Roxbury, owned horses and a chaise and kept two indentured servants. One of these, a man named Cuffee, ran away and Smybert inserted an advertisement in the Boston *Gazette*, for October 3/10, 1737, asking for his return. The artist mentioned that his servant could be identified by the leather breeches he wore, "stained with divers sorts of paints."

After Dean Berkeley returned to Ireland, he became the Protestant Bishop of Cloyne. He wrote to Smybert, urging him to join him there, but the artist preferred to remain in Boston where he died in 1751. He was buried in the Granary Burial Ground.

John Singleton Copley
1738-1815

John Singleton Copley
ᘓ 1738-1815 ᘒ

PAUL REVERE sat at the workbench of his silver shop at 50 Cornhill, Boston, opposite the old State House. In his left hand, he held a silver teapot of his own design and manufacture. His right elbow rested firmly on the workbench, his hand supporting his chin, as he gazed resolutely before him with dark, piercing eyes. His auburn hair was neatly brushed and tied with a ribbon in back; he wore a blue-green waistcoat over a full-sleeved white linen blouse. This was how John Singleton Copley, the artist, saw the great patriot in 1765 and painted his portrait. Paul Revere was thirty years of age at the time; the artist was twenty-seven years old.

Born of poor Irish parents in 1738, in Boston, Copley displayed a talent for drawing at an early age. When his father died, his mother, Mary, who conducted a tobacco shop on Long Wharf where she sold, "Virginia Tobacco, Cut, Pigtail and spun, of all sorts," married Peter Pelham, painter and engraver. The latter had a son named Henry, about the same age as young Copley. Shortly after the marriage, they all moved ". . . into *Lindel's* Row, against the Quaker's Meeting House, near the Upper End of King Street, Boston," where Mary Pelham continued her occupation as tobacconist.

The Pelhams worked hard to support themselves. In addition to the tobacco business, John's stepfather added to his meager earnings as an artist by giving writing lessons, guidance in fancy needlework and dancing lessons. In spite of lingering puritanical warnings against such dalliance as dancing, the ladies and gentlemen of Boston persisted in improving their dance steps, the better to perform at the balls held by the English governor of the Colony at Province House, where the latest in English modes and manners were presented to an admiring circle of wealthy merchants and their ladies.

It is not known definitely who young Copley's teachers were, but it is believed that he studied the copies of the Old Masters hanging in Smybert's studio and it is also possible that he received some instruction from Smybert himself. In addition, he must have learned a great deal about art from his stepfather, who was soundly trained in painting and engraving. Whatever his art education, John Singleton Copley was painting well by the time he was sixteen years of age and he had reached a state of perfection in his work when, in 1765, he painted Paul Revere.

At this period Copley also completed a portrait of Henry Pelham called, *A Boy with a Flying Squirrel*. It was taken to London by a friendly sea captain named Bruce, who showed the picture to Sir Joshua Reynolds. The famous English artist pronounced it, ". . . *a very wonderful performance* . . . by a young man who was never out of New England and had only some bad copies to study." Reynolds sent the picture, with one of his own, to the April–May, 1766, exhibition of the Society of Artists, held at Spring Gardens, London, where it was favorably received. Benjamin West, the American artist who was living in London, liked the painting so much that he proposed Copley for membership in the Society, where he was duly elected as a Fellow.

Captain Bruce urged Copley to come to Europe. "Should

you take that resolution," he wrote, "I may venture to assure you that you will meet with much encouragement and patronage." But Copley elected to remain in America a while longer.

In 1769, Copley married the daughter of Richard Clarke, a wealthy tea merchant for the East India Company. They lived in the Clarke house, ". . . a two-story brick mansion, with dormer windows. . . . In front was a small courtyard." John Trumbull, a fellow artist—and a descendant of Priscilla and John Alden—described Copley at the time of his marriage as ". . . a handsome figure in powdered wig, dressed in a suit of crimson velvet with gold buttons . . ."

Graced with a natural ease and elegance in his manner of living, Copley was doing so well that he could afford extravagances to which he was naturally inclined and which he felt necessary to his position as Boston's leading painter. In writing to a friend in London at this time Copley remarked: "I make as much as if I were a Raphael or Correggio . . ."

The famous and the fashionable of Boston, including those distinguished patriots and Signers of the Declaration of Independence, John Hancock and Samuel Adams, came to Copley's painting rooms in the Clarke mansion to sit for their portraits. He was also called to New York to carry out several commissions.

The artist was a methodical worker, lavishing his skill in reproducing exactly the rich textures of the costumes worn by his clients. His portraits were spirited likenesses of some of our greatest statesmen and of brave women who encouraged their men in freedom's cause.

The principle of liberty was running strong in the colonies the night of December 16, 1773, when the patriots boarded ships of the East India Company in Boston Harbor and jettisoned the cargoes of tea consigned to Copley's father-in-law, as agent for the Company. It was a trying situation for the artist and his family for Copley's sympathies were with the colonists. Although a grave crisis had been reached between England and the colonies, Copley believed that the problems between the two countries would soon be resolved. He, therefore, made plans for a long period of study abroad and in June, 1774, sailed alone for Italy, by way of England.

Copley was warmly received in London by Sir Joshua Reynolds and his compatriot, Benjamin West. While there he fulfilled some portrait commissions and began pictures of the King, George III and Queen Charlotte for completion at a later date. In late August he set out for Italy.

His letters to his wife and friends were filled with admiration for the treasures he saw during his Italian trip. "Art is in its utmost perfection here," he wrote, "a mind susceptible of the fine feelings which art is calculated to excite, will find abundance of pleasure in this country." But beneath this happy mood, Copley was becoming increasingly aware that war was imminent between England and her colonies across the Atlantic.

On July 22, 1775, he wrote to his wife from Italy: "Whoever thinks the Americans can be easily subdued is greatly mistaken; they will keep their enthusiasm alive until they are victorious. You know, years ago, I was right in my opinion that war would be the result of the attempt to tax the colony. It is now my settled conviction that all of the power of Great Britain will not reduce them to obedience." Knowing that when war came, there would be no market for portraits at home, he urged his wife to join him in England. "Should I now return to America," he wrote to her, "I should have nothing to do, and I cannot think of going back to starve with my family."

Mrs. Copley and the two children, Elizabeth and John Singleton the Second, were reunited with the artist in December, 1774, in England. Copley opened a studio at 25 George Street, Hanover Square, London, where he was immediately successful as a portrait-artist and as a painter of dramatic and historical subjects which included *A Youth Rescued from a Shark*, and *The Death of Chatham*.

Copley and West were present in the House of Lords on the historic day, December 6, 1785, when George III, in a speech from the throne, formally received and recognized the United States of America as a sovereign nation.

Shortly before this occasion, Copley had all but finished a portrait of a fellow countryman, Elkanah Watson. In the background of the picture, he had placed a ship, shown under full sail for America, carrying the first news of the King's recognition of America's independence—an action he was convinced would be accomplished.

Hurrying back to his studio after the King's speech, Copley picked up his brushes and, as Elkanah Watson related the incident, ". . . there with a bold hand, a master touch, and an American heart, attached to the ship the stars and stripes! This was, I imagine, the first American flag hoisted in old England, on canvas!"

Copley died in London in 1815.

Gilbert Stuart
1754-1828

Gilbert Stuart
1754 - 1828

On an autumn evening in 1795, a lank, attractive man in his early forties came to the door of the Presidential mansion in Philadelphia. He was wearing a dark blue jacket, black knee breeches, white stockings, and silver buckled shoes; he carried his hat under his arm; his long hair was brushed back over his ears. His arresting face, usually relaxed, was now tensely set.

The visitor, who had felt at ease in the presence of English royalty, experienced a sudden lack of composure as he entered the house to be received by the First President of the United States. But if the caller, Gilbert Stuart, had any doubt about his reception that evening, his fears were soon dispelled by the warm and friendly manner of his host. Noticing his guest's arrival in the candle-lit room, George Washington came to his side immediately and cordially introduced him to the assembled company.

Stuart had come to Philadelphia to paint the President on order of Samuel Vaughn of London, who in February, 1785, had presented a beautiful Italian marble mantelpiece to Washington for the banquet hall at Mount Vernon. Washington and Vaughn had never met, but the former's idea of government had appealed strongly to the Londoner, as it had to so many people in the world, and he desired Washington's portrait.

The goal of every American artist, and several foreign ones

too, was to paint Washington, and the President complied in most instances. "I am so hackneyed to the touches of the painter's pencil," he once wrote to a friend, "that I am now altogether at their beck; and sit, 'like Patience on a monument,' while they are delineating the lines of my face."

Stuart was better qualified than any of the applicants to paint Washington's likeness. He was the most sensitive and capable artist in the colonies and a man of intelligence and charm as well.

"I was born," he would jokingly say, "in a 'snuff-mill' in Rhode Island." But the truth was that his father, also named Gilbert, operated a snuff-mill near Wickford, Rhode Island, on the Narragansett River, for Dr. Moffatt, a fellow-Scotchman. The father prospered sufficiently to build himself a house and marry. Three children were born to the Stuarts, Gilbert, Ann and James. The youngest did not live for long.

Gilbert was born in 1754. At the age of thirteen he had begun to copy pictures, the usual procedure followed at that time by beginners in art. When he was eighteen he began formal instruction in drawing with Cosmo Alexander, a Scotch painter, who lived in Newport. In 1772, Stuart was taken to England by Alexander, but the latter died, leaving Stuart with no means of support. The following year the young artist made his way back to Newport, completely destitute.

The handsome, spirited, though sometimes melancholy youth became the friend and companion of Benjamin Waterhouse, also of Newport. Waterhouse's goal was medicine, but he was also interested in art. The two young men would sometimes engage a husky blacksmith of the town to pose for them, doing careful life drawings of their muscular subject.

At this time, also, Stuart taught himself to play on various musical instruments. "Gibby," his friend Waterhouse remarked, "became enamoured with music. . . . I was willing to believe that he was knowledgable in the science of sweet sounds, but I did not always feel them so sweetly as he did."

When Waterhouse left for England in March, 1775, to further pursue his medical studies, Stuart was disconsolate. The departure of his good friend had left him without anyone with whom he could discuss and plan his hoped-for career as an artist.

A few months later, with very little money in his pocket, the impulsive Stuart made his way to Boston, where he succeeded in arranging passage on the last ship to sail from America for England before the Revolutionary War called a halt to such intercourse. This was on June 7, 1775, ten days before the battle of Bunker Hill. On the eve of sailing, Stuart stood beneath the window of a young lady whom he had admired during his Boston stay, serenading her on a flute.

Arriving in London penniless, Stuart was soon re-united with Waterhouse, who arranged lodgings for him near his own quarters, where his needs could be properly looked after.

Stuart was finally admitted, as an apprentice, to the painting rooms of Benjamin West. Ever willing to serve his fellow countrymen, West generously arranged for the impoverished Stuart's care and instruction. It was in West's studio that Stuart met John Trumbull, who was also serving the American master as an apprentice.

After a long period of study, West advised Stuart that he was now capable of competing with professional artists and urged him to begin a career of his own.

While he was considering this move, Stuart was approached by a Mr. Grant, a Scotch gentleman of means, who commissioned the young artist to paint his portrait in a fashionable standing pose. Stuart accepted the order with some misgiving, as he was uncertain of his ability to handle the full figure.

When Mr. Grant arrived for the first sitting, he remarked that the day was more ideal for skating than posing for a picture, to which the artist wholeheartedly agreed. Without further ado, artist and model went gaily off to the near-by Serpentine River, where they cut all kinds of fancy capers on the ice, to the great amusement of other skaters. Returning to the studio, Stuart decided to paint Mr. Grant in a jaunty skating pose against a wintry landscape, instead of in the conventional pose originally intended.

The painting caused quite a stir when it went on public exhibition in 1783, at Somerset House, London. The daring arrangement of the pose and the excellency of its execution evoked praise for the artist. The jovial Grant, attending the exhibition one day dressed in the costume he wore while posing for the picture, was besieged by crowds of visitors who exclaimed: "There is he! There is the gentleman!" This was too much for Grant and he departed hurriedly from the gallery—yet not without a secret measure of delight, we suspect, at being recognized by the public. The success of the Grant portrait had its effect and Stuart soon found himself one of the most sought after artists in London.

His method of painting differed from that of other artists. Once he had the personality of the sitter firmly in mind, Stuart worked rapidly, laying the paint on in direct, loose strokes, a method that gave a quality of freedom to his work. He seldom touched an area, once it was in place. It was his practice to make a likeness omitting the eyes until the very last thing. Stuart contended that the character of the individual depended on a correct analysis of the nose, rather than of the eyes. The color of his portraits was clear and vibrant. "Good flesh coloring," he said, "partook of all colors, not mixed, so as to be combined in one tint, but shining through each other, like blood through the natural skin."

With a handsome income from portrait painting now assured, Stuart began to expand his mode of living. He staffed a fine house with servants and entered upon a lavish social life. In 1786, he married the daughter of a Dr. Coates, in London. His bride managed somehow to keep up with the excessive entertainments Stuart gave frequently. These were attended by the gayest and wittiest members of London society.

Stuart's extravagances, however, could not keep pace with his earnings, and in 1788 he left for Ireland to escape his creditors. He established himself in Dublin, where his fame as an artist had preceded him, and he was once more sought after as a fashionable portrait painter. But his continued inability to manage his own affairs caused a repetition of the London situation; consequently, in 1793, he sailed with his family to New York, in the hope of bettering his fortune in the newly founded Republic.

Soon after his arrival in New York, Stuart opened a studio in Stone Street, near William Street, where he painted members of the Yates family and John Jay, the first chief justice of the United States. It was Jay who arranged the first meeting between Washington and Stuart, in Philadelphia, then the Federal Capital.

On the appointed morning in early September, 1795, George Washington came to Stuart's painting room at Fifth and Chestnut Streets, in Philadelphia, to sit for the Vaughn portrait. Instead of the blue and buff uniform in which he sometimes posed for other artists, the General, on this occasion, was dressed in the black velvet suit he wore as President. His hair had been freshly arranged with a be-ribboned queue and powdered, by his barber. He walked into the room with characteristic quick steps and resigned himself "to the painters chair." Stuart began work on the first of three pictures from life he was to paint of Washington between the years 1795 and 1796. These were to serve as models for all future portraits he painted of the President.

Some time during the summer of 1796, Stuart bought a house and stone barn at Germantown, near Philadelphia. He turned the barn into a studio. It was there that the two succeeding paintings of Washington were made from life, one a head and shoulders arrangement, the other a full length portrait depicting the President standing with right arm and hand extended, the left hand clasping a sword. The latter picture was ordered by the Marquis of Lansdowne of London.

Early in 1797, the year in which Washington resigned the presidency to return to Mount Vernon, he wrote the following lines in his journal: "1797, January (7) Wind at No. West and cold with clouds. Road to Germantown with Mrs. Washington to see Mr. Stuart's paintings." On the occasion of this visit, Washington paid Stuart a rare compliment by stating that he would pose for him whenever he wished. But the opportunity never again presented itself—two years later General Washington was dead.

Stuart continued his residence in Germantown until 1805, when he moved to Boston, where he remained until his death in July, 1828.

One of the finest painters produced in America, Stuart will be remembered not only for his revealing portraits of the First President, but also for his distinctive paintings of many of the nation's founders.

George Inness
1825-1894

George Inness
1825-1894

"A landscape painter's day is delightful. He rises early, before sunrise, at three in the morning, and sits under a tree and watches and waits. There is not much to be seen at first. Everything has a sweet odor. Everything trembles under the freshening breeze of the dawn. Bing! the sun gets clearer; but he has not yet torn away the veil of gauze behind which lie the meadow, the valley, the hills on the horizon. Bing! Bing! The first ray of the sun! . . . another ray! . . . the landscape lies entirely behind the transparent gauze of the ascending mist gradually sucked up by the sun, which permits us to see as it ascends, the silver-striped river, the meadows, the cottages, the far-receding distance. At last you can see what you imagined at first. Bam! The sun has risen . . . The flowers lift up their heads. The birds fly here and there. The rounded willows seem like wheels on the river's edge and the artist paints away."

Corot

IN the early part of the nineteenth century the wild and mountainous region in the vicinity of West Point attracted the attention of two painters, Thomas Cole and Asher Durand. Unlike their predecessors, who were chiefly concerned with portraiture, these artists concentrated on landscape, which they painted realistically. As pioneers, along with Thomas Doughty, of the American landscape movement, Cole and Durand literally lived the life of explorers in their search for paintable subjects. They went forth on painting trips with the

39

zeal and enthusiasm of adventurers, packing their art supplies on their backs and often reaching their objectives only after enduring much physical discomfort. Cole related with some amusement how on one painting expedition he plunged through the ice in crossing a deep mountain stream and did not find shelter and warm clothing until he reached a remote mountain inn, later in the day, though he managed to keep his art supplies dry while struggling to reach shore!

The historic name, Hudson River School, was applied to the work of these men, inspired by the location where they painted their majestic landscapes.

George Pearce Inness, the son of Scotch parents, who was to follow in the footsteps of these Hudson River School artists and eventually transcend their achievements, was born on May 1, 1825, near Newburgh, New York, not far from West Point. That same year the Inness family moved to New York City, traveling in a sailing sloop down the Hudson River with all their belongings aboard. In 1830, the family settled in Newark, New Jersey, where Inness attended school.

During his boyhood, Inness received instructions in painting from a journeyman artist named Baker, whose teaching methods consisted in allowing the boy to copy pictures he had painted. Except for this experience, and a short period of study later on with Regis Gignoux, in New York, Inness received no further lessons in art.

When he was sixteen years of age, Inness became apprenticed to a map maker in New York. During this time he progressed in his drawing and studied the paintings to be seen in the windows of the elegant art stores on Broadway. Here were to be found, among other things, landscapes by artists of the Hudson River School.

The grand aspects of nature which these men had painted

in exact detail made a strong impression on Inness. He began working in this manner, but his health would not permit long, fatiguing trips to the Catskills and Highlands of the Hudson, where Cole and Durand had obtained some of their finest views. He chose, instead, the quiet surroundings of the New Jersey countryside, where he could emulate the technique of his favorite painters without undue exertion.

By 1844, Inness, then nineteen years of age, had progressed well enough in his painting to have one of his landscapes accepted for exhibition by the National Academy of Design. This was the institution founded in 1826, in New York City, by the artist-inventor, Samuel Morse, and others, to encourage and develop American art.

The official recognition of his work by the Academy led to the inclusion of paintings by Inness in other exhibitions; and resulted also in the purchase of his paintings by collectors—at modest prices. This was an extraordinary testimonial to be received by an artist who was still so youthful. These few sales encouraged Inness. He was hopeful that he would soon earn enough from the sale of pictures to finance a period of travel and study abroad. He felt keenly the need of such a trip, as no opportunities existed in New York, at that time, to see original paintings by the Old Masters—the traditional source of inspiration for every artist.

In 1847, the wish of the eager artist was fulfilled through the generosity of Ogden Haggerty, a New Yorker, who, on learning of the young man's ambition, furnished him with funds to go to Europe. This was to be the first of four journeys Inness was to make to Europe between the years 1847 and 1870, with Italy as the principal objective each time.

From about 1850, the artist's manner of painting underwent a new and steady development. His former adherence to a complete imitation of nature slowly gave way to a free interpretive style, decidedly more in keeping with his fine intellect and spiritual sense. Inness once declared: "The true use of art is . . . to cultivate the artist's own spiritual nature. . . ." This was a devotion that possessed him completely as he contemplated nature's changing moods.

Inness found delight in painting the American landscape, and fortunately there were plenty of art patrons who shared his enthusiasm for it. As his reputation grew, the number of collectors acquiring his work increased, providing a handsome income for the artist in his later years.

In 1850, Inness married Elizabeth Hart, his second wife.* Three years later, he was elected an Associate of the National Academy of Design. Meanwhile, he had been abroad again, reveling in the abundant art treasures to be found there. Upon his return home, he lived in Brooklyn for a time, then settled in New England.

He chose Medford, Massachusetts, as his home, entranced by the broad vistas of landscape he found in the surrounding countryside. When war was declared between the States, Inness, in a burst of patriotic fervor, organized a band of militia to follow the flag, but the emotional shock of war was too overwhelming for his poetic soul, and he suffered a physical collapse.

When the war ended, Inness bought a fine house in Montclair, New Jersey, where he lived with his family in comfortable style. He also maintained a studio in New York.

He occasionally accepted invitations to visit various parts of the country, where he was warmly received by his admirers. He traveled as far as California on one such trip, stopping enroute to see the wonders of the Yellowstone.

* *Inness's first wife, Delia Miller, died soon after their marriage.*

GEORGE INNESS

Inness's style of painting, which he referred to as "poetic realism," had a popular appeal. Frederick Stymetz Lamb, a painter friend, described Inness's artistry in this way: "As others were realists in fixed states of nature, so Inness was a realist in the moods of nature . . . the early spring, the misty morning, the changing color of the fall; the greens of summer, the frosty morning were a joy to him, and he revelled in their difficulties. There have been poets, there have been painters, but few painter-poets that achieved his success."

The man who translated nature's moods into idyllic paintings, among them *Peace and Plenty* (1865), *The Coming Storm* (1878) and *Indian Summer* (1894), was of average height, slender, with strong features and penetrating eyes. He wore his hair long and sported a Dickens-type beard. He was intelligent and personable, generous to a fault, and at times excitable, particularly when he was talking on the subject of painting, which was nearly all of the time.

Lamb told how Inness, on one occasion, responded to a young painter's solicitation to visit his studio and criticize his work. "When Inness arrived," Lamb stated, "he rushed at once to the sketches and started to give his theories of painting. . . . He spoke of color combinations, demonstrated methods of brushwork and finally set aside both brush and palette. Taking his thumb, he drew the color together with a few marvelous sweeps—as was often his habit—then excitedly seizing his friend by the lapel of his coat, he explained the reason at the same time leaving beautiful color combinations on the Sunday coat!"

During a visit to Scotland in 1894, Inness was fatally stricken on August 3, at the Bridge-of-Allan, where he had gone to view the sunset.

James McNeill Whistler
1834-1903

James McNeill Whistler
᎒ 1834-1903 ᎒

JAMES McNEILL WHISTLER's first objective in life was to
become a soldier. His father, George Washington Whistler,
had served in the American army for years, with the rank of
Major, therefore it seemed fitting that the son should follow in
his father's footsteps. But beneath this military urge, there persisted a fondness for art which eventually absorbed the young
man's complete interest.

Whistler entered the United States Military Academy at
West Point, July 1, 1851, with every intention of winning a
commission. As his education progressed, however, he began
to lose interest in his studies, except for drawing—a subject he
continued to pursue with unusual vigor.

"The rough sketches by Whistler," his instructor, Robert
W. Weir, asserted, "exhibit decided talent and singular independence of thought." However, Colonel Robert E. Lee, then
Commandant at West Point, was unimpressed by Cadet Whistler's artistic accomplishments. When he failed to pass his final
examinations in June, 1854, Whistler was dismissed from the
Academy. In later years he recalled that he had stated in the
final chemistry examination that silicon was a gas. "Had silicon
been a gas," he added, "I should have been a Major-General."

Whistler was born on July 10, 1834, at Lowell, Massachusetts. When he was nine years of age he accompanied his

mother and brothers to Russia, where his father was engaged by Czar Nicholas I to build a railroad from St. Petersburgh to Moscow.

During his stay in St. Petersburgh, which lasted until the death of his father in 1849, James Whistler attended the Imperial Academy of Fine Arts. Returning to America that same year, he completed his preparatory schooling, then entered West Point.

After his removal from the Military Academy, Whistler worked briefly drawing maps for the U.S. Coast Guard and Geodetic Survey. This job ended when an unsympathetic boss fired him for decorating the borders of the maps with drawings of strange characters!

In 1855, Whistler left for Paris to study art, completely unaware that he was destined to spend the rest of his life abroad. The gay, positive "Jammie," as he was called by his mother, plunged into the art life of Paris with rollicking enthusiasm. Short of stature, of slender build and with black curly hair, the jaunty American, who was given to eccentric dress, laughed and joked his way into the hearts of the French people.

The four years Whistler spent in Paris were not given over entirely to frivolous escapades, however. He enrolled in the studio of Charles Gleyre where, subsequently, Claude Monet and Pierre Renoir studied. These two artists, together with Edouard Manet, were later to make painting history as the leaders of the impressionistic movement.

Gleyre, a painter of "antique dreams" clung to the academic belief that the exact imitation of nature was the ideal in painting. Many of his students, however, inspired by the new movements in art then developing in Paris, began to adopt different views. They haunted the galleries of the Louvre Museum, seeking among the more loosely painted pictures by the

Old Masters, new ways to free themselves from academic restraint.

Whistler, who had joined the younger artists in their "revolt," turned to the paintings of Titian and Velasquez, where he found the elements of style he desired to form his own manner of painting.

One of the first pictures by Whistler to reveal a personal style of painting was called *At the Piano*. It is an interior view, with two figures. These were posed for by his half-sister Deborah (Mrs. Seymour Haden), who is seated at the piano, while her little girl Annie stands opposite, in the curve of the instrument. The picture, revealing contrasting values of black, white, and gray, was submitted to the Paris Salon of 1859. Apparently, this representation of familiar life appeared too commonplace for academic tastes and the painting was rejected, along with Manet's first entry to the Salon, *The Absinthe Drinker*. Through the sympathetic understanding of the artist, Francois Bonvin, however, some of the rejected pictures were displayed at his studio, and the public was invited to view them. The exhibition was visited by Gustave Courbet, the famous realist painter, who had warm praise for Whistler's picture.

Soon after this exhibition, Whistler moved to London. He presently rented his London quarters to George du Maurier, illustrator and fellow-student under Gleyre, who later became famous for his novels, *Trilby* and *Peter Ibbetson*. Whistler took temporary lodgings at Wapping, on the lower Thames where he began a series of etchings of this colorful and romantic shipping center. The resulting prints, sixteen in all, became known as *The Thames Series*.

During the next few years, Whistler divided his time between Paris and London, joining his friends at every opportunity, to discuss the course of artistic events in the two capitols.

His knowledge of art affairs and his ready wit made him a popular figure at these gatherings, where one of the main topics of conversation was how best to achieve recognition for the new art movements.

When, in 1863, Whistler's *The White Girl* was turned down by the Paris Salon, in company with Manet's *Luncheon on the Grass* and other pictures, the independent artists protested to the Emperor over their continued rejection by the Salon, whose juries firmly believed that no art was good art unless it conformed to rigid academic requirements. This, in the final analysis, meant doing nothing original. After hearing their protest, the Emperor issued a decree, allowing the rejected artists to hang their paintings in the same building where the official Salon was being held.

The art critics and the public flocked to the "Salon des Refuses," to laugh and jeer at the "new art," singling out Manet's painting for their choicest invectives. Whistler's painting also received its share of adverse criticism, though one lone reviewer bravely called it "a morsel full of flavor."

The White Girl was a daring conception for its time. The informal pose of the white-gowned, red-haired model (Joanna Heffernan), shown against a white-curtained window to receive the full effects of the light—and loosely painted—was a radical departure from the crisp pictorial style favored by the conservative Salon painters.

In 1863, Whistler returned to London, where he rented a small house at 2 Lindsey Row, in Chelsea, on the Thames River. It was a picturesque part of the city, where, among other landmarks, Old Battersea Bridge could be seen, looming up in the river mists in typical Japanese print fashion.

Whistler's mother came from America to live with her son in Chelsea. Born Anna Mathilda McNeill, daughter of Dr.

Charles McNeill, of Wilmington, North Carolina, this gentle, southern lady presided over her son's little house with patient understanding.

The artist's studio was located on the second floor of his residence in Chelsea. It was a small room, with gray painted walls, black doors, and a black baseboard. The simplicity of the room was relieved by a number of colorful Japanese prints hanging on the walls.

During his student days in Paris, Whistler had shared the interest of the impressionists in Japanese prints. The ability of the Oriental print makers to obtain effects by the simplest means stimulated him to try for similar results in his own work.

The White Girl was among the first canvases he painted in this fashion. It was followed by other pictures, including the notable portraits of his mother, Thomas Carlyle and Miss Alexander. In these compositions Whistler demonstrates quite clearly his enthusiasm for Japanese prints. This influence is obvious in the use of modified silhouette shapes against simple backgrounds and in the careful attention given to the designing of the space areas around the figures.

Portrait of the Artist's Mother, completed in 1871, was first shown in the Royal Academy exhibition held the following year. It had been accepted for hanging only after a vigorous defense of the painting had been made by Sir William Boxall, the only member of the jury to recognize its outstanding qualities. Because of this incident, Whistler never again contributed paintings to the Academy exhibitions.

Mrs. Whistler was sixty-seven years of age when she sat for her portrait. It must have been something of an ordeal to pose for her son, as Whistler was well known for the long, exhausting sittings he demanded of his models.

When Thomas Carlyle, the Scotch philosopher and

writer, was being painted by Whistler, he found posing for him a slow and tedious task. On one occasion, as he was leaving Whistler's studio after a particularly long day in the painter's chair, he met young Cicely Alexander entering the house. Inquiring the purpose of her visit, she replied, "I am going to be painted by Mr. Whistler." The weary Carlyle smiled wryly and remarked, "Puir lassie, puir lassie!" The Carlyle portrait fared no better in public interest than the *Portrait of the Artist's Mother*. Both pictures, painted within a year of each other, remained unsold.

F. R. Leyland, the shipping magnate of Liverpool, ordered portraits of himself and his family from Whistler. The commissions came at a welcome time, as the artist's finances—never prosperous—were now at a very low stage. In addition, Leyland bought Whistler's picture, *The Princess of the Land of Porcelain*, depicting a standing figure wearing colorful Japanese robes, to grace the wall above the mantelpiece in the dining room of his London house.

When Whistler saw the painting hanging on the gloomy, if expensive, leather-covered wall of Leyland's dining room, he asked permission to do a simple decorative scheme to enliven the picture's setting. Leyland granted the artist's request and left London soon after for a long summer holiday, never dreaming that Whistler would carry the "simple decorative scheme," far beyond the limits mutually agreed upon!

Without further consultation with Leyland, the artist decided to enlarge the original plan of design into a more ambitious project. Using the forms of peacocks and details of their plumage as decorative motifs, he presently became enthusiastically involved in re-decorating the entire wall space. By the end of summer, the Leyland dining room fairly glistened with variations of what Whistler called, "Gold upon Blue, Blue upon Gold." He was so delighted with the results he was achieving on the project that he invited his friends in to watch the progress of the work.

When Leyland returned to his London house at the end of summer, he was horrified at what he found there. *The Princess of the Land of Porcelain* stood as serenely as ever above the dining room mantelpiece, but the leather-covered walls of the room were alive with the designs of peacocks! Indignant over what he considered a shocking abuse of friendship, Leyland refused to pay Whistler the full amount that he asked for the work. Whistler retaliated by painting on the end wall a peacock grasping gold coins in its claws (to represent Leyland), while another bird standing near by in an attitude of dignified disdain portrayed the artist.

In 1877, the year after the decorating of the Peacock Room, Whistler exhibited some of his finest pictures at the Grosvenor Gallery in London. Included in the exhibition were the portraits of Thomas Carlyle and Miss Alexander; and *Nocturne in Black and Gold: The Falling Rocket;* a view of fireworks bursting over Cremorne Gardens, opposite Chelsea. He believed that this exhibition, representing years of hard work, would result in many sales. On the strength of this belief —and the expected payment in full of the Leyland-Peacock Room commission—Whistler had contracted to build a new house in Tite Street.

But the run of hard luck begun with the Leyland episode continued through the Grosvenor exhibition. Ruskin, the noted art critic, who disliked Whistler and his work, wrote a damaging review of the show. He singled out *The Falling Rocket,* for particular scorn, saying, "The ill-educated conceit of the artist nearly approached the aspect of wilful imposture. I have seen and heard much of cockney impudence before now, but never expected to have a coxcomb ask two hundred guineas for flinging a pot of paint in the public's face."

Stung by this unjust criticism, Whistler, in 1879, brought suit against Ruskin. He won a verdict of one farthing, but he was made to pay the considerable court costs and lawyers' fees.

Meanwhile, the effects of Ruskin's harmful review and other critical stories on Whistler's exhibition were beginning to have their effect on conservative British opinion. Due to mounting resentment against Whistler, fanned by a hostile press, it was no longer fashionable to collect his pictures, or to be painted by him. He was finally forced to declare himself bankrupt in 1879.

His new residence on Tite Street, the interior decorated in yellow and blue, was sold with all of its furnishings to satisfy his creditors. Virtually without funds, Whistler turned to print making to earn what money he could.

The Fine Arts Society of London, realizing his predicament, sent him to Venice to do a series of etchings. He spent fourteen months on the assignment, working directly with an etcher's needle on small copper plates he carried around in his pockets.

Whistler had a difficult time making ends meet in Venice. A friend who found him there was disturbed over his impoverished condition. When this friend suggested that a tear in the artist's hat be mended, Whistler proudly remarked, "A darn is premeditated poverty, but a tear is the accident of a moment!"

Returning quietly to London in 1880, Whistler tried out the Venice plates, selecting twelve to be printed for distribution to members of the Fine Arts Society.

The critics were soon aware of Whistler's return to London. Whenever his work appeared in exhibition, it was received by them with the same feeling of contempt that had marked their previous comments. But Whistler had had enough of critics. From this point on he answered their charges publicly, through the newspapers, maintaining a continuing debate with them, which he relished hugely—and the public also seemed to enjoy. Most of the letters and criticisms were published later by Whistler under the title, *The Gentle Art of Making Enemies*.

In 1881, Whistler's mother died. This same year her portrait was shown for the first time in America, but no museum or collector offered to buy it at a reputed price of $1200. The painting was returned to the artist in 1882.

At the age of fifty-four, Whistler was married for the first time to Mrs. Beatrix Godwin, the widow of E. W. Godwin, who had designed the artist's house on Tite Street.

The consistent fight waged by Whistler and his contemporaries through the years against the narrow confines of academic control in art was beginning to have its rewards. The new artists were not only being honored in official circles, but their productions were being received with greater favor by the public.

In 1889, and again in 1891, Whistler was awarded decorations by the French Government for his art; and in 1891, also, France (prompted by Georges Clemenceau who was an ardent follower of the new art movements) purchased *Portrait of the Artist's Mother* for the Luxembourg Museum in Paris. This same year, the *Portrait of Thomas Carlyle* was bought by the Glasgow Art Gallery, and in the following year a successful exhibition of Whistler's work was held in Paris. These pleasant occurrences, added to the affection he had always had for Paris, prompted the artist to make his home there.

In 1892, the Whistlers rented a fascinating old house at 110 Rue du Bac, painting the entrance green and white and enlivening the interior with color. They furnished the place with choice antique pieces, old silver, and a rare collection of Chinese blue and white porcelain. It was a perfect setting for an artist, and one to be happily shared and enjoyed by their many interesting friends.

With the sudden illness of Mrs. Whistler, the agreeable Paris days drew to a close. Abandoning Paris, Whistler accompanied his wife to Lyme Regis, near London, where he hoped the climate would restore her health. In May, 1895, Mrs. Whistler died.

Shortly after the death of his wife, Whistler moved back to Chelsea, where, except for an occasional visit to the Continent, he remained until his death on July 17, 1903. He was buried beside his mother in the old graveyard at Chiswick.

Winslow Homer
1836-1910

Winslow Homer
1836-1910

BREVET MAJOR GEORGE WARD NICHOLS, attached to
General Sherman's command, gave a vivid account of the military spectacle being enacted almost daily during Sherman's
historic march to the sea.

"All day long," he wrote in his diary, "the army has been
moving through magnificent pine woods . . . the savannahs
of the South, as they are termed. I have never seen, and I can
not conceive a more picturesque sight than the army winding
along through these grand old woods. The pines, destitute of
branches, rise to a height of eighty or ninety feet, their tops
being crowned with tufts of pure green. . . . In the distance
may be seen a group of horsemen—some General and his staff
—turning about here and there, their gay uniforms and red and
white flags contrasting harmoniously with the bright yellow
grass underneath and the deep evergreen . . . nothing can be
more delightful nor can there be more beautiful subjects for
the artist's pencil than a thousand sights which have met my
eye for days past, which can never be seen outside the army.
There is by the way, a most excellent artist accompanying the
expedition, who is working for the Harpers."

The old *Harper's Weekly* magazine hired trained artists,
among them Winslow Homer, to cover the War between the
States for its readers. Nothing escaped the roving eyes of these

skilled draughtsmen. The clumsy maneuvering of the raw recruits; the hour of bivouac and thoughts of home; the fateful time of battle—these were some of the things the magazine artists saw and drew with keen perception.

Winslow Homer served as war artist for *Harper's* from 1861 to 1864. He was assigned to the Virginia Campaign, but participated in no major engagements, although he witnessed several skirmishes.

Homer's ability to record his observations quickly and accurately was a facility he possessed from childhood, a probable inheritance from his mother, who was an amateur flower painter of distinction.

Winslow Homer was born in Boston, February 24, 1836. When he was six years of age, the family moved to Cambridge, where Homer and his two brothers, Charles Jr., and Arthur Benson, grew up in pleasant surroundings. Near by were expansive meadows in which the children played such games as Crack the Whip, or indulged in such pastimes as Waiting for a Bite, in the deep pools of the brook.

Homer, an alert, studious boy, attended Washington Grammar School in Cambridge. His parents had planned to send him to Harvard College, but a reversal in the family fortunes prevented this.

While still in his teens, "Win," as he was known to his family, became apprenticed to John H. Bufford, a Boston lithographer, at a salary of five dollars a week. After two years of humdrum work, Homer quit the Boston job to become a contributor to *Harper's Weekly*, in New York. This magazine agreed to take whatever drawings of current interest he produced, an arrangement that gave him more time to devote to his avowed purpose of becoming an artist.

On his arrival in New York, the short, slender young man,

neatly dressed and wearing a wisp of a moustache, took lodgings in a rooming house at 128 East Sixteenth Street. Two years later, he moved to the old Gothic towered New York University Building on Washington Square, where Samuel Morse and George Inness once had studios. It was in this building that Morse tinkered with the telegraph instrument, an invention that was to bring him greater fame than his position as the university's professor of the literature of the arts of design.

Homer took quarters high up in one of the towers, occupying a space described by one of his friends as being "remarkable for nothing but its contracted dimensions." But just outside his windows was a low lying roof, where he could pose models to study the effects of light upon them. Homer's interest in the correct use of light in painting was as intense as that of his contemporary, Thomas Eakins.

When Lincoln was inaugurated as President, Homer was sent to Washington by *Harper's* to sketch the event. This was at a time when photoengraving was unknown and an artist was employed instead of a cameraman to make pictures of newsworthy events. The artist's drawings were transferred to wood blocks, cut out by expert wood engravers, and printed. The material gathered by Winslow Homer during his war reporting experiences was reproduced by *Harper's* in this way.

Some of these sketches were utilized by the artist in fashioning his early paintings, in which the force of "the winds of battle" was vividly emphasized. Among these pictures, *Sharpshooter* (1862), *A Skirmish in the Wilderness* (1864) and *Prisoners from the Front* (1866) show the artist's special capacity for seizing the drama of the event and making of it an unforgettable subject. Homer, now in his early thirties, was devoting more of his time to serious painting and less to illustration.

He had learned the rudiments of painting from an obscure

artist in New York named Rondel, developing with amazing speed and dexterity in the use of materials and techniques, under the guidance of his instructor. In what seems an incredibly short period of time, Homer's work was being shown in various exhibitions.

The war scenes were followed by a series of romantic oils in which ladies of fashion were depicted toying delicately with croquet mallets, *Croquet Scene* (1866); or bearing themselves as gracefully as possible while horseback riding as in *The White Mountains* (1868); or viewing "the beautiful sea" from a safe vantage point atop the sand dunes in *Long Branch* (1869).

Subsequently, Homer painted a number of pictures which represented some of the nostalgic scenes of his boyhood. *The Berry Pickers* (1873) and *A Fair Wind* or *Breezing Up* (1876) are charming examples of this reminiscent mood. In the latter painting, one can see indications of the intensely accurate seascapes he was to accomplish in later years.

Trim and debonair, always immaculate in speech and dress, Homer's appearance in metropolitan art circles gave no hint of a man who enjoyed an active outdoor life. Yet he made frequent trips to the Adirondack Mountains and the Canadian wilds, dividing his time on these excursions between his favorite sport, fishing, and capturing the characteristic atmosphere of the woods in a number of clear, crisp water-color paintings. This was a medium in which he seemed to delight.

Some of the impressions made on these trips were developed into oil paintings. *The Two Guides* (1876) and *Huntsman and Dogs* (1891) are the best known of these accomplishments. While in the north woods, Homer was impressed by the impenetrable silences of man and nature, a diversion that his own personality sometimes required to keep an even balance.

In 1876, Homer went to Virginia to paint episodes of Negro life. He was the first artist to interpret the wholly expressive moods of a naturally happy people. He joined the Negroes at work and at play and in the silence of devotion, with a deep affection for religious beliefs which he represented with such tender feeling in the painting *Sunday Morning in Virginia* (1877).

Homer's peak of greatness, however, lay in the magnificent paintings he made of the sea during the last twenty-five years of his life.

Born of a long line of down-Easters, no one could paint the sea with greater feeling. In his lonely studio at Prout's Neck, Maine, where he finally chose to retire, Homer was in daily communion with the sea. He often kept the long hours of vigil with the fisherman's wives as they gazed anxiously out to sea through a thundering northeaster. He sometimes accompanied the fishermen on their runs along the coast, experiencing events on these trips that resulted in such paintings as *The Gale* (1883), *The Herring Net* (1885), *Eight Bells* (1886) and *Kissing the Moon* (1904).

Homer was a realist, painting truthfully what he saw. Once he had fixed the mood of a theme, he applied his brush strokes vigorously to the canvas, laying on thick notes of color occasionally to point up the dramatic impact of a subject.

Now and then, Homer would leave his Prout's Neck retreat for a winter in Florida, or the Caribbean, where he was immediately attracted to the long stretches of sandy shores and the relentless pounding of the sea.

From the numerous water colors and drawings Homer made on these holiday trips, he developed his paintings, *The Gulf Stream* (1899) and *Searchlight, Harbor Entrance, Santiago De Cuba* (1901).

A confirmed bachelor, Homer enjoyed the seclusion of his studio at Prout's Neck, where he could work undisturbed on the significant contributions he made to American art. Winslow Homer died there on September 29, 1910. He was buried in Mount Auburn Cemetery, Cambridge, Massachusetts.

Thomas Eakins
1844-1916

Thomas Eakins
1844 - 1916

As a young man, Thomas Eakins often accompanied his father Benjamin on hunting and fishing trips to the Cohansey Marshes at Fairton, New Jersey, off the Delaware River. These occasions not only provided pleasant hours of companionship between father and son, but they afforded young Tom an opportunity to observe what Walt Whitman called, "Nature's calm content," and to build up within him that wealth of inspiration that later was to spread itself on canvas.

Born on July 25, 1844, in Philadelphia, Thomas Eakins grew to manhood in the city of his birth, married and remained there throughout his life, except for the years of study abroad and brief visits to adjacent cities and the Far West.

The artist's youthful years, spent within a family of culture and deep affection, were ideally happy ones. The elder Eakins, a writing master, gave every possible encouragement to his son, who, like all boys, was passionately fond of sports, but unlike most growing lads, had a mind equally devoted to intellectual accomplishments.

Upon graduation with honors from Central High School, Eakins entered the Pennsylvania Academy of Fine Arts, a musty old building with a leaky roof, filled with an indifferent collection of paintings and a group of plaster casts presented the Academy by Napoleon I. To relieve the monotony of cast drawing, the students occasionally pooled their pocket money to pay for a "live" model who, properly chaperoned by the Academy curator, struck heroic poses for the students to draw.

But Thomas Eakins's chief delight was attending the lectures in anatomy given by Dr. Joseph Pancoast at Jefferson Medical College, a tangent he considered absolutely necessary to his development as an artist. At the age of twenty-two, skilled in drawing and anatomy, Eakins sailed for Europe for advanced studies in Paris.

Soon after his arrival in Paris, Eakins enrolled in the classes of Jean Leon Gerome, whose "patient study of nature" appealed to his sense of perfection. Gerome was a thoroughly competent technician and, though dry as dust in his own painting, he had the ability to bring to light the best that his students possessed. A feeling of mutual esteem developed between teacher and pupil which greatly encouraged Eakins.

Unlike Whistler, who wore foppish clothes and busied himself with art events of the day, Eakins went his quiet way, paying little attention to his personal appearance or needs and remaining totally indifferent to the current upheavals taking place in the art world.

Tall, lithe, with deeply tanned face pierced by flashing dark eyes, his black hair cut in crew style, Eakins appeared to be a young man with a purpose as he moved through the Paris scene.

But his seriousness of manner was sometimes relieved by flashes of gaiety. He frequently joined his friends for evenings of merriment at a favorite cafe, or engaged in horseplay with his fellow students at the school.

His letters home were filled with the enthusiasm of a young man who is happily and hard at work, but still mindful of the sacrifices his parents had made for him. "I have tried to act in moderation," he wrote to his father on one occasion, "without being liberal like a poor man or mean like a rich one." After three years of devotion to the formal study of art, which included work in sculpture under Dumont and additional training in painting with Leon Bonnat, Eakins went to Spain.

The Spanish journey, which lasted for six months, opened up new horizons to Eakins, whose analytical mind forever sought to perfect his own approach to painting. The works of Rembrandt, Velasquez, and particularly Ribera, stirred him deeply, and the keen observation he gave to their work was his first move away from the influence of his teacher Gerome.

"I am painting all the morning," he wrote home at this time, ". . . I am very well, and it seems to me when I breathe the dry warm air, and look at the bright sun, that I never was so strong . . ."

This strength of spirit imparted itself to his painting, which had taken on a new vitality through the intense study he was making of the Old Masters.

He had begun work on an oil painting—the first one he had attempted outside of Gerome's class—posing a trio of street musicians in the open air. "Picture-making is new to me," he wrote to his family, "there is the sun and gay colors and a hundred things you never see in a studio light, and ever so many botherations that no one out of the trade could ever guess at."

However, Eakins had learned his trade well. *Street Scene in Madrid,* the subject of this first picture, was a remarkable achievement for one so young. There is nothing of Gerome in this canvas. Instead, there is an impression of the Eakins that is to come, carefully and sensitively observant, suffused with the spirit of the masters of painting that he had looked upon in the art galleries of Spain.

Returning to America in 1870, Eakins rejoined his family in Philadelphia. He fitted up a studio on the top floor of his parents' house on Mt. Vernon Street and began his professional career.

Members of Eakins family and friends were his first models. His father and his two sisters, Margaret and Caroline; Mrs. James W. Crowell and her daughters, Katherine and Elizabeth; were among the relatives and friends who posed for Eakins at this time. The penetrating analysis of character and detail that was to establish Eakins as the greatest of American realists demonstrated itself in these early pictures.

Five years after his return home, Eakins painted the celebrated *Gross Clinic*, for the Jefferson Medical College, where he had studied anatomy. This was his first important commission and one that brought ridicule upon him for the literal treatment of its theme. Hailed by some critics as the greatest figure painting yet produced by an American and condemned by others as a gruesome subject, the picture remained in obscurity until 1878, when it was finally purchased by the College for the meager sum of $200. This was the first of many bitter disappointments Eakins was to experience in his lifetime.

During his studies with Gerome, Eakins followed the current doctrine that insisted that a painting, to be structurally correct, must have as its foundation a well-defined drawing upon which the color was to be meticulously applied. This technique was in the full tradition of David and Ingres, who were still held as the authorities in the Paris Salon circle. But the impact of the Old Masters convinced Eakins that the classic approach to painting was static and that the only way to give a fluid tempo to the stilted style taught by Gerome was to draw directly with the brush. He found this method to be the true expression of the painter and one which allowed a most complete expression of the use of the paint medium.

Eakins was never considered a brilliant colorist. Greatly intrigued by the play of light on objects, he went so far as to prepare small models of figures and objects to be used in his paintings so that he might study them in natural light, in order to achieve the correct tones. This method was first used in the preparation of his rowing pictures, painted between 1871 and 1874, among them *The Biglen Brothers Turning the Stake* (Cleveland Museum of Art) and *Max Schmitt in a Single Scull.*

On his return from Europe, Eakins resumed his hunting and fishing trips and the athletic exploits of his boyhood. He believed most emphatically in the old adage, "a sound mind in a sound body," and went frequently to the Schuylkill to row or to the Delaware for a day of sailing.

Eakins began his teaching career at the New Pennsylvania Academy of Fine Arts in the late 1870's. But due to the refusal of the overseers to permit mixed models to pose before the students, Eakins resigned from the Academy in 1886. At the urgent request of some of his students who quit the Academy in protest with him, Eakins agreed to criticize their work in an art class they had established outside the Academy. He refused to accept any remuneration for this activity, however.

In 1889, he was commissioned to do a testimonial portrait of Dr. D. Hayes Agnew, the noted professor of surgery at the University of Pennsylvania, who was retiring from his post. Eakins created an impressive composition, depicting Dr. Agnew in the operating room, explaining to students the course of the operation he is performing. This picture was enthusiastically accepted by the undergraduates of the Medical School, who presented it to the University. Outside the University, however, it was not to fare any better than *The Gross Clinic.* The painting was barred from an exhibition by the

Society of American Artists and was refused hanging as an invited work by the officials of the Pennsylvania Academy in 1891. So Eakins, who had paid no attention to the discussions being waged in art circles during his Paris days, now found himself the center of an artistic maelstrom in his own city.

American art lovers of this period had become stranded in the sentimental shallows of the French Salon. That Eakins chose to paint the commonplace and familiar scenes of everyday life was an unheard-of barbarity. The artist found himself fighting for his vital realism almost singlehanded against the apparently immovable weight of what is known as academicism.

During the 1890's Eakins painted *Taking the Count, Salutat* (Phillips Academy, Andover, Mass.) and *Between Rounds*, documentary expressions of incidents familiar to devotees of boxing. They were painted after the artist had witnessed hundreds of rounds of boxing, a further indication of the care he exercised in achieving his strong realism.

At the turn of the century, Eakins painted the portraits of *Addie* and *Clara*, two exceptionally impressive studies. The latter was eventually to find its way to France, after the artist's death—as a gift of the Philadelphia Museum of Art to the Louvre, in 1931.

From 1900 until ill health forced him to stop painting altogether, Eakins concentrated, with few exceptions, on figures and portraits. The spiritual portrait of *Cardinal Martinelli* and the assertive portrait of *Signora Gomez d'Arza* were both painted in 1902. Many appraisers of American art look upon these two pictures as milestones in the development of our native art. These paintings were followed by many more notable productions until death came to still Eakin's hand in June, 1916.

THOMAS EAKINS

The passing of Thomas Eakins brought into full significance the genius of a man who, with indomitable courage, had remained true to his philosophy of art. All his life Eakins had fought steadily uphill, his eyes fixed on the bright star of truth. Time has proved the merit of his search.

Mary Cassatt
1844-1926

Mary Cassatt
ᘛ 1844-1926 ᘚ

WHEN Mary Cassatt announced to her wealthy and socially prominent parents, at the age of twenty-three, that she wished to become an artist, her indignant father remarked, "I would almost rather see you dead." But, being a strong willed young lady, Mary Cassatt was allowed to have her own way.

Born in Allegheny City, Pennsylvania, on May 22, 1844, Mary Cassatt's childhood was spent with her parents abroad, except for occasional return visits to their Philadelphia home. She was later to take up permanent residence in France.

In 1864, she enrolled in the Pennsylvania Academy of Fine Arts, where she studied drawing for a year, returning to Paris in 1866, with the avowed intention of making art her career.

Mary Cassatt followed the practise of all beginning artists at that time, by copying the paintings of Old Masters. Afterwards she took advance studies in painting with the French artist, Charles Chaplin, in Paris, and with the Italian painter and engraver, Carlo Raimondi, in Parma. When she was twenty-eight, her picture, *On the Balcony*, painted in Seville, was exhibited in the Paris Salon of 1872.

Her appreciation of the Italian masters—Correggio and Parmigiano particularly—was reflected in the strong drawing and color she gave to her early work. This led Degas to exclaim, when he saw one of her paintings for the first time in the Salon of 1874, "There is one who feels the way I do."

Mary Cassatt was a frequent contributor to the Salon exhibitions until 1876, when the impressionist movement, to which she had become attached, absorbed her complete interest.

The impressionist movement was formally presented in an exhibition held in Paris in 1874. Not to be confused with the Salon of the same year, with its usual drab, colorless studio concoctions, the impressionist exhibition sparkled with color and life.

The realist writers, Duranty and Zola, had been urging the artists to find their subjects outside the studios, in the life about them. "I have seen," Duranty said, "a form of society, various actions and events . . . comedies of gesture and countenance that were truly paintable. . . . Everything appeared to me arranged as if the world had been made expressly for the joy of painters, the delight of the eye."

This newly discovered world thrilled the young painters, but baffled the public, who had come to the impressionist's exhibit to see the artists interpretations of the things favored by Duranty and Zola.

Théodore Duret felt impelled to explain the new artists' methods. "The impressionist," he wrote, "paints without hesitation upon his canvas water which has this, that, or the other hue. The sky is overcast, . . . he paints water that is milky, heavy, opaque; the sky is clear, he paints the water sparkling, silvery, with an azure sheen. . . . The sun goes down and darts its rays along the water, the impressionist . . . dashes upon his canvas yellow and red. . . . Certain clayey soils in the country take on a lilac tone, the impressionist paints lilac landscapes. Under a summer sun in the shade of green leafage, the skin and clothes take a violet tint, the impressionist paints violet people in the woods. Then the public lose all self-control and the critics shake their fists. . . . They do not take the pains to see if what they see painted corresponds or not to what the painter has really seen in nature. . . . The impressionist's work does not look like the work of the painters that went before him . . ."

Although Mary Cassatt was not invited to exhibit with the impressionists until some time later, she was enthusiastic over their productions and bought a number of their paintings, urging her friends to do likewise. When Degas asked her to join the group and exhibit in the fourth impressionist show, held in 1879, she accepted with delight. "Now I could work with absolute independence," she remarked, "without considering the opinion of a jury. I had already recognized who were my true masters. I admired Manet, Courbet and Degas. I took leave of conventional art—I began to live." *La Loge*, and *The Cup of Tea*, the latter a portrait of Mary's sister Lydia, now the property of the Metropolitan Museum of Art, were shown in the 1879 exhibition.

As a refined American lady, living comfortably in Paris, Mary Cassatt could not wholly subscribe to Duranty's views that an artist should try, "to catch all the different aspects of life." She chose, instead, to picture the genteel ways of living, leaving the mundane subjects for the penetrating analysis of the men painters.

The artist concentrated on portraits and figures in her work, laying particular stress on the mother and child theme in her figure painting. Her portraits, never commissioned, were of women seen in a box at the opera, having tea, reading, or engaged in the frivolous occupation of arranging a veil.

As a master craftsman, Mary Cassatt was positive of her medium, laying the brush strokes down with surety and purpose. She is known especially for the radiant play of light she obtained in her pictures.

During her studies under Raimondi, Mary Cassatt learned the art of print-making, a technique she pursued briefly again in 1891. Influenced by Japanese prints, she made a series of ten etchings in color, employing the flat decorative style of the Japanese artists, to illustrate a lively succession of women's activities, including the inevitable tea party.

The artist's family and friends visited her frequently, and she often joined them on trips to Italy and Spain, her favorite countries, outside France. In 1901, while on a tour of Spain, she discovered three of El Greco's finest paintings, *The Assumption of the Virgin, View of Toledo* and *The Inquisitor.* Through her urging, these pictures were acquired by friends, and eventually found their way into American collections, along with other significant art treasures Mary Cassatt had entreated them to buy. She was responsible for the formation of more important private collections in America—including the Havermeyer Collection in New York—than any one person.

In 1904, the artist was made a Chevalier of the Legion of Honor and in 1909 she was elected an associate of the National Academy of Design, an honor which she refused.

During the First World War, Mary Cassatt, now partially blind, stayed at Grasse, in the south of France. At the war's end, she returned to the Chateau Beaufresne, in the Oise, near Paris, which she had purchased in 1893. She died there, on June 14, 1926.

Albert Pinkham Ryder
1847-1917

Albert Pinkham Ryder
1847-1917

"The starred and stately nights seemed haughty dames in jeweled velvets, nursing at home in lonely pride the memory of their absent conquering Earls, the golden helmeted suns!"

Herman Melville, *Moby Dick*

ALBERT PINKHAM RYDER was born on March 19, 1847, in New Bedford, Massachusetts, not far from the Spouter Inn, where Herman Melville stopped to gather material for his book, *Moby Dick*. As a boy, Albert had often watched the schooners drift down the Acushnet River, bound out for Nantucket and ". . . the wild and distant seas where the whale rolled his island bulk."

When Ryder accompanied his parents to New York in 1870, to live with an older brother, the winds and the sea and the sometimes aching loneliness of the shore were etched deep in his memory. He had come to New York, a tall, shy, neatly dressed youth of twenty-five, wearing a thin red beard, and possessed with the desire to become an artist. But when he applied to the school of the National Academy of Design for admission, he was refused on the grounds that the ill-drawn studies he submitted were not acceptable.

This rejection from the Academy school was a bitter disappointment to Ryder. He had suffered from bad eyesight from childhood and feared that his affliction might one day end his

83

dream of becoming an artist.

Fortunately, at this time Ryder made the acquaintance of William E. Marshall, a portrait painter, who realized the young man's plight and gave him every encouragement. Under Marshall's guidance, Ryder again applied for admission to the art school and was accepted.

In the meantime, Ryder had left home to make his own way as an artist, completely unaware of what such a move entailed. "The artist needs but a roof, a crust of bread, and an easel," he said, "and all the rest God gives him in abundance." With this simple declaration of faith to guide him—practically all he possessed—Ryder began his painting career.

His studio was a small, crowded room, where he sometimes worked far into the night, creating the poetic images he required in his paintings. If his efforts to achieve certain results were unsuccessful, Ryder went on walks about the city, searching "the starred and stately nights" for effects to use in his pictures. When he sold his first painting for a modest sum, he ran all the way down town to bring his father the good news.

Alone in his room, Ryder went happily about the business of picture making, entirely oblivious of time and personal needs. He would become intrigued by what he called the "inner light," laboring to achieve this effect in his painting by working and reworking transparent glazes of color over his pictures. When he considered a painting finished—a rare occurrence with Ryder—it glowed with a delicate luminosity through the use of this involved technique.

Ryder admitted that he could not paint directly from nature. "In my desire to be accurate," he once said about his attempt at landscape painting directly from nature, "I became lost in a maze of detail. Try as I would, my colors were not those of nature. . . ." Later, alone in his studio, Ryder envisioned the same landscape once more: "The scene presented itself one day before my eyes. . . . It stood out like a painted canvas—a deep blue of a midday sky—a solitary tree, brilliant with the green of early summer, a foundation of brown earth and gnarled roots. Three solid masses of form and color—sky, foliage and earth—the whole bathed in an atmosphere of golden luminosity; I threw my brushes aside; they were too small for the matter at hand. I squeezed out big chunks of pure moist color and, taking my palette knife, I laid on blue, green, white and brown in great sweeping strokes. As I worked I saw that it was good and clean and strong. I saw nature springing into life upon my dead canvas. It was better than nature, for it was vibrating with the thrill of a new creation. Exultantly I painted until the sun sank below the horizon."

Unfortunately, Ryder did not exercise the care necessary to assure the permanency of his work. Full of the joy of painting, he failed to realize that in mixing certain colors together, there might be a resultant chemical reaction that would darken and sometimes crack the paint at some future time. Also, he was not aware that some of the media he used to thin his colors would cause the paint to pull away from the picture's surface. A good many of his paintings have suffered irreparable damage because of this lack of technical knowledge.

Ryder received few visitors, as he preferred to work undisturbed in his little studio. On one occasion he permitted an art student to stop by to show his sketches. When the young man asked him if he thought his things would sell, Ryder remarked, "You bring that in like a twist in a pig's tail. I cannot sell my pictures. I had an auction once and they brought a dollar or two. . . ."

In 1873, one of Ryder's paintings was invited to the spring exhibition at the National Academy of Design. But, it remained for Daniel Coltier, recently arrived from London to open a decorating shop in New York, to understand the true worth of Ryder. Learning that the artist and some of his fellow exhibitors had had their work refused by the jury for the Academy exhibition of 1875, Coltier displayed their paintings in his store. He and his partner Inglis bought some of Ryder's pictures and also commissioned him to decorate some leather screens, mirrors and cabinets. One of Ryder's friends said of these furbelows, "I remember one mirror with a border of roses, very lovely." The shy, good-natured Ryder was overcome by the many kindnesses shown to him by Coltier and Inglis. "They had a marked influence on my career," he said.

In 1883, Ryder went to England with Coltier on his first trip abroad. He later joined a sculptor friend for a tour of the Continent. When some one asked Ryder on his return what he thought of the many Old Masters he had seen hanging in the art galleries abroad, he remarked that they were "merely painters." He had not meant this remark in a disparaging way, but only as a means of saying that, as an imaginative artist, he was not interested in a literal translation of things, as the Old Masters were.

Ryder was now exhibiting more frequently and his work was beginning to receive favorable reviews, but he was too occupied with his painting to pay much attention to such things.

As he grew older, Ryder retired more within himself, keeping to his cluttered bachelor quarters where, dressed in overalls and wearing carpet slippers, he shuffled about, fussing over his paintings. He continued to see his old friends, sometimes joining them at dinner, or for an evening at the opera. On these occasions he would dress in formal clothes, which he carefully preserved in an old trunk.

But his little studio room was where he enjoyed being

most of all. There was an old garden outside his windows, ". . . whose great trees," he said, "thrust their green-laden branches over the casement sills, filtering a network of light and shadow on the bare boards of my floor. Beyond the low roof tops of neighboring houses sweeps the eternal firmament with its ever-changing panorama of mystery and beauty. I would not exchange these two windows for a palace with less a vision than this old garden with its whispering leafage."

In 1902, Albert Pinkham Ryder was named an Associate of the National Academy of Design and four years later he became a full Academician. J. Alden Weir painted a portrait of Ryder for the occasion. He was delighted to receive these honors from his friends. It seemed that a poem he had written years before had actually come true:

> Who knows what God knows?
> His hand He never shows,
> Yet Miracles with less are wrought,
> Even with a thought.

Ryder's health remained good until 1915, when the years of privation began to take their toll. He died on March 28, 1917, at Elmhurst, Long Island, where he had gone to spend his remaining days with friends.

This artist of "the tragic landscape" had bequeathed to us in such paintings as *The Forest of Arden, Toilers of the Sea, Macbeth and the Witches* (Phillips Memorial Gallery, Washington, D.C.) and *The Race Track* (Cleveland Museum of Art) some of the most sensitive creations in American art.

John Singer Sargent
1856-1925

John Singer Sargent
❧ 1856-1925 ❧

JOHN SINGER SARGENT had none of the financial problems
most artists have to face. Born in Florence, Italy, on January 12,
1856, the son of Dr. Fitzwilliam Sargent and Mary Newbold
Sargent, he was raised in an atmosphere of comfort and culture.

His American parents, who preferred living in Europe,
took their son with them on various trips about the Continent,
finally establishing their residence in Paris. At the age of eighteen, John Sargent who had previously studied drawing in Italy,
entered the studio of Carlus-Duran, in Paris.

This master, reputed to be one of the best portrait painters
in France, was a skilled technician who, according to an enthusiastic admirer, ". . . makes arranged portraits in which
glitter the lustre of the whites, the fire of the reds, the gold of
the yellow, the lazulis of the intense blues, in which satins shim-
mer and velvets tremble."

Upon completion of his studies with the Paris master,
Sargent left for Spain to study Spanish painting. He was particularly inspired by the works of Velasquez, whose technique
made the deepest impression on him, as it had on Whistler and
Eakins.

In May, 1876, at the age of twenty, Sargent, although an
American citizen, made his first trip to America, visiting relatives in Philadelphia and Newport. He returned to Paris in

October and the following year sent his first picture to the Paris Salon, a practise he followed annually until he gave up his Paris home.

Sargent remained on the Continent until 1884, traveling extensively through France, Spain, Italy and Holland, finally removing to London, where he engaged a house once occupied by Whistler at 31 Tite Street, in Chelsea.

A tall, well-built man, wearing a Prince Albert style beard, "worldly in appearance, manner, and speech," Sargent seemed cool and aloof to casual acquaintances. But beneath this formal reserve existed a warmth of heart that asserted itself generously when he was among his friends. He never married.

One of the most widely sought after portrait painters of his time, Sargent was besieged by people clamoring for sittings and interviews. On occasions when the pressure upon his time and energies became too great, he would quietly slip away to the Continent, where he would indulge himself in landscape painting for a few weeks. He would be seen at these times, dressed in old clothes, his sleeves rolled up and a faded cap pulled over his eyes, happily painting away in some sunny Italian square or catching the morning sun as it fell on distant mountain peaks in the Austrian Tyrol. He gaily bantered with the native people as they stopped to watch him at work on these excursions.

When he appeared in his London studio to paint a client, however, John Sargent assumed an imperious manner that few people dared to penetrate. He was complete master of the situation always, warning the sitter that he must not look at the picture while it was in progress, then, *remaining completely silent*, Sargent proceeded with his work.

The artist was a superb painter, working as one critic remarked, "With a technique unparalleled in our day for swiftness, surety, and brilliance, he has shown us exactly what his sitters looked like bedecked and surrounded with comforts and luxuries of life." But Degas and Whistler had other ideas about Sargent's talents. They believed that "he could not rise above the fashionable Salon painters of his time." On the other hand, Sargent was warm in his praise of the work of both Degas and Whistler.

Among the notables painted by Sargent was Robert Louis Stevenson, who was living at Bournemouth. Sargent visited him in 1884, and again in 1885, painting the author in two informal poses which are among the artist's most accomplished works. One is inclined to believe that these were the kind of pictures Sargent preferred doing, instead of engaging in what he termed, ". . . the routine of portrait painting with anxious relatives hanging on my brush."

But in his portraiture, according to a London critic, "Two of the very best examples of the finest period are his portraits of Asher Wertheimer and the Misses Werthimer. . . . Neither of course, has the qualities of a Rembrandt or a Velasquez. . . . But if his work be compared with that of Raeburn, Reynolds or Gainsborough, it will be found that he can hold his own with anything but their very best. . . . No painter paints with such certainty and directness."

In 1890, Sargent was engaged to paint the murals in the Boston Public Library. He chose the History of Religion for his theme, traveling to Egypt and Jerusalem to make studies for the decorations. This commission was finally completed in 1916. In 1916 also, Sargent was given the job of decorating the rotunda of the Museum of Fine Arts in Boston, which he completed in 1925. He was also commissioned to do the Widener Library murals at Harvard University.

Sargent made frequent trips to the United States to attend

to his various assignments, but he faithfully returned at intervals to his London home. He, along with Whistler and Mary Cassatt remained an expatriate until the end.

John Singer Sargent died on April 15, 1925, in his house in Chelsea.

Maurice Prendergast
1859-1924

Maurice Prendergast
1859-1924

WHEN Maurice Prendergast was a child he owned a dog. There was nothing unusual about this, but there was something exceptional about the color of his dog. When the town clerk, to whom he had gone to buy a license for his pet, asked him to describe the color of the animal, Maurice replied without hesitation, "He is a purple dog," leaving the bewildered clerk to ponder how in tarnation a dog could be of purple hue! But this was no problem to young Prendergast who, hoping to be an artist one day, saw things quite differently in the fancied world of color in which he lived.

Born in St. Johns, Newfoundland, in 1859, of poor Scotch-Irish parents, Maurice was brought to live in Boston by his parents when he was two years old. He received his formal education at Rice Grammar School, on Dartmouth Street, and upon graduation found a job selling yard goods in a Boston dry goods store. When time permitted, he made drawings of the textile designs, coloring the patterns he drew with washes of brilliant hues.

Every Sunday he would pack a lunch and hike with his brother Charles to the countryside near Boston. Here he would sketch everything that took his fancy—especially cows—which seemed to interest him more than anything else at that time. Brother Charles said in later years that, "Maurice was death on cows."

Maurice soon left the dry goods store to work for a sign painter long enough to learn the trade, then he set to work on his own, painting signs at twenty-five and fifty cents apiece. At the end of five years he had saved a thousand dollars, which he thought would be enough money to finance his art studies abroad.

In May, 1884, Prendergast, now twenty-six years of age, arrived in Paris, happy as a lark. He took lodgings on the Rue Campagne Première, in a fine-looking old house where other artists lived. A big sunny balcony hung over a courtyard where the artists gathered to exchange news of the art world. Prendergast liked the informal atmosphere immediately.

After he was settled, Prendergast enrolled in Carlo Rossi's school, later moving over to the Julien Academy, where he registered for half-day sessions in the life class. He had never worked from the model before and his first efforts at drawing were awkward. His instructor, Jean Paul Laurens, looked over his shoulder one day and gruffly told him that he should take up a trade instead of art. But the young man persisted in his efforts and, in a short time, was drawing as well as anyone in the school.

His mornings were spent in the art classes, but his afternoons were devoted to the study of life in the city—the cafes, the parks, and the teeming boulevards where he could sketch and perfect his knowledge of form and movement.

One day when he was sketching on one of the boulevards a man stopped to watch him at work. When Prendergast finished the picture, a water-color painting, the stranger insisted upon buying it. Prendergast could not quite believe that such good fortune could happen to him.

By extraordinarily careful management, Prendergast stayed in France nearly five years on his meager savings. He returned home with many sketches and water colors, penniless but happy. He went to live with his father and brother Charles, in a narrow white frame house at Winchester, near Boston. Here he resumed his sign painting and undertook what illustration work he could find, for money was scarce in the Prendergast household—and in Boston picture buyers were even scarcer.

When he finally sold a painting from an exhibition his old father remarked, "Well, all the fools are not dead yet." But this parental displeasure fortunately had no effect on the young artist's painting. He went on with his work just the same, encouraged by his brother Charles, who contributed what he could from his meager earnings as a frame maker, so that Maurice could continue to paint.

Whenever he had time to do so, Prendergast was off to sketch at Salem Willows or Revere Beach, favorite resorts near Boston, walking part of the way to save carfare. On these occasions, he developed a style of painting that was based upon the impressionistic practices of his Paris days, realistic in effect but without attention to minute detail. Although a skilled draughtsman, he allowed only the barest essentials of drawing to appear in his pictures, depending upon color rather than drawing to define the forms.

Prendergast managed to visit France briefly again in 1892. In 1898 he made a third trip abroad, arranged by Mrs. Montgomery Sears, one of the few people in Boston who believed in his future as an artist. This time his objective was Italy, with visits to Rome, Florence and the hill towns. Finally he settled in Venice for a stay of several months.

During his student days in Paris, Prendergast became fond of the paintings by Carpaccio, the Venetian old master who painted scenes of life in Venice with a lively sense of color.

And now Prendergast was in the midst of the real thing, with the same colorful fêtes and religious processions going on around him. It was as though Carpaccio's paintings had suddenly come to life.

Prendergast liked Venice. The gay spirit of the people seemed to reflect his own happy mood at being among them. He spent part of each day sitting at a table in a sidewalk cafe, sketching the people as they moved around St. Mark's Square. In the evening he would occupy a table at Florian's with other artists, smoking long black cigars and looking on enchanted while the table rocked under the repeated blows of his companions as they drove home their arguments on art.

He spent long hours in the art galleries, faithfully studying the paintings by the Venetian masters. "The work of the grand Venetians makes me ashamed to call myself an artist," he wrote to his brother Charles. But in Venice he set eagerly to work, painting, among other things, the busy and colorful Ponte della Paglia, opposite the Bridge of Sighs. The flow of movement and vibrant patterns of color Prendergast achieved in this picture recall his admiration for the paintings of Carpaccio.

Near the end of his stay in Venice, Prendergast was taken seriously ill. When he was well enough, he wrote to his brother Charles, "It is too bad for your sake I am sick. It would be so fine to be home in the old studio, helping you along with the frames. We together were such a fine team. . . ." But there was no cause for alarm, and Maurice was soon able to join his brother in Winchester.

Home again, Prendergast resumed his painting trips to the seashore, including Marblehead in his itinerary. He also began to look upon Boston, with its tree-lined streets and quaint old red brick houses, as a new discovery for the interpretation of his art.

On one occasion he was commissioned to paint a picture of a church on Cambridge Street, in Boston. The thing that interested him about the church was its faded blue-green door. He went about the business of composing the picture as he wanted it to be, leaving the door as the very last color note to be laid down in the picture. When the time came for this final touch, a house painter arrived on the scene and painted the door a raw, vivid blue!

While Maurice was pursuing his painting, Charles was carving away at his frames. He had finally earned enough to move from Winchester back to Boston, where the brothers rented a studio at 50 Mt. Vernon Street, but their financial situation was still far from secure.

In 1901, Maurice Prendergast received the bronze medal for water-color painting at the Pan-American Exposition, held in Buffalo. It was the first official award he had ever received and a major triumph, for until now his work had been observed with derision by most art critics.

From that year on, the artist's trips to New York became more frequent. He preferred this city to Boston and hoped that one day he would be able to live there. During these visits Prendergast toured the city, choosing subjects to paint. Central Park was one of his favorite sources of material. On one occasion there he came upon a May Day fête, a scene vibrant with the movement of gaily dressed children and fluttering ribbons against the fresh greens of spring. He liked the scene so much that he made a water-color painting of it. He also painted scenes of children riding happily on the park's carousel. Prendergast enjoyed painting pictures with children in them.

Meantime, the artist was showing his work in various exhibitions. In 1905, he showed at Kimball's Gallery in Boston and at the Macbeth Gallery in New York, where a group of his

Venetian pictures was shown. Robert Henri saw the paintings and invited Prendergast to participate in the now historic exhibition of The Eight,* held in 1908, in the same gallery. Prendergast liked the excitement caused by such events, which he felt could only happen in a city like New York.

By a stroke of good fortune, Charles received an order from a Philadelphia insurance company for twelve carved frames. Maurice did what he could to assist his brother with the order and in due time the job was finished. Charles received $1800 for the order. Winding up their affairs in Boston, the two brothers made a brief trip to Europe, then returned home to settle in New York.

They found just the place they wanted to live, on the third floor of an old house at 50 Washington Square South, near the building where Winslow Homer once resided. Charles took over the duties of the household, working so hard at keeping the place clean that Maurice urged him not to dust so much, since the dirt only settled down again, anyway. Maurice took turns about the square for exercise, hurrying back to the studio when this chore was done to resume his painting. The brothers made a fine team!

This change of scene was just the thing for Maurice Prendergast. Though museum directors and collectors generally did not clamor for his work, a few discerning ones did. In 1915, Joseph Brummer gave Prendergast a fine big exhibition at his gallery and some sales were made. His work was also beginning to appear in the important national exhibitions.

Prendergast was living in an atmosphere where much was happening, and he could join his friends among The Eight whenever he wanted to for a good dinner and spirited conversation at one of the many restaurants they frequented near

* *See chapter on Robert Henri.*

by. It was like Paris or Venice all over again. His deafness, which had started when he was young and had by now worsened, did not stop him from enjoying the discussions. "If they're saying anything nice, they yell loud enough for me to hear," he said. "I hear only the best of everything."

In 1923, Prendergast won the third William A. Clark Prize of $2000 and the Corcoran Bronze Medal for his oil, *Landscape with Figures*, shown in that year's Corcoran Biennial Exhibition, in Washington, D.C.

Maurice Prendergast died on February 1, 1924, in New York City. His devoted brother Charles was disconsolate over his passing. "We'd been together so many years, I don't know what to do," he said.

Robert Henri
1865-1929

Robert Henri
ᘯ 1865-1929 ᘯ

ONE day in 1884, while delivering milk to a customer in Atlantic City, New Jersey, James Albert Cathcard, a dairyman, came upon a surprising sight. Covering an entire rear plaster wall exposed by workmen who were engaged in remodeling the customer's house was a series of freshly painted, well executed drawings that had not been there the day before. Curious as to the originator of such skilled decoration, Cathcard, himself a one time art student, discovered that they had been made by Robert Henri, the eldest son of the family he was serving. Struck by the young man's drawing ability, Cathcard agreed to give him what instruction he could. Later, he advised Robert's parents to send him to the Pennsylvania Academy of Fine Arts, in Philadelphia.

The Henris originally hailed from Cincinnati, Ohio, where Robert was born on June 24, 1865. While still a boy, he and his younger brother were taken by their parents to Nebraska, where the father purchased a cattle ranch. The two boys pitched in to help their parents operate the ranch, often sharing the sometimes dangerous duty of standing guard over the fertile lands to prevent trespassing by unscrupulous roving cattlemen and their herds. After a series of family misfortunes, the Henris gave up their western holdings and moved East, finally settling in Atlantic City.

When Robert Henri enrolled at the Academy in Philadelphia under Thomas Anshutz, the successor to Thomas Eakins at the school, his experiences in the West had made him a completely self-possessed young man. Eager to be on his way to an art career, Henri lost no time at his studies and in 1888, when he left for Paris, he was well prepared to take up advanced courses in drawing and painting.

Arriving in Paris, Henri enrolled in the classes conducted by William Adolphe Bouguereau, the unrivaled exponent of "the classic line and academic figure," who was then the rage in academic art circles. During his formal studies with Bouguereau, Henri kept an eye on the direct painting methods being practised by the impressionists, sensing that this technique would be more to his taste than following his teacher's method of painting, which consisted of making a complete drawing of a subject on canvas before applying the paint.

Turning to the collections seen in the Louvre, Henri looked for pictures by the Old Masters whose style was obtained by direct painting. He found what he wanted in the productions of Velasquez, Hals and Goya, finally developing a characteristic manner of painting of his own, based on these sources. After further independent study in Italy and Spain, Henri returned home in 1891, to accept a teaching job at the Women's School of Design, in Philadelphia.

In this city, Henri made the acquaintance of several newspaper artists, including John Sloan, George Luks, William Glackens and Everett Shinn. As Shinn explained it, these artists of the press "were called upon to cover everything that is caught by the modern camera in the twinkling of an eye." They were painters as well, but because of the commonplace nature of the things they painted, their work attracted no attention in official art circles, where they wished to be recognized.

Henri became the friend, mentor and champion of these artists and his studio at 806 Walnut Street was their weekly meeting place, where endless discussions were held to resolve their situation. Henri taught in Philadelphia for four years. Two more trips to Europe followed.

When Henri returned from Europe in 1900, to settle down to work and teach in New York, he found the art world still dominated by narrow, conservative elements. Few opportunities existed for artists of advanced thinking to exhibit publicly and no progressive art teaching was being offered in the schools.

After a while, Henri joined the staff of the New York School of Art, taking over the men's life class. He immediately put into effect his radically different views on art teaching and his theories on art in general. "Everything in life is a subject," he told his students, "but it is not the subject that counts; it is what you yourself bring to it." He urged his pupils to stop making their pictures appear "lifeless as a cabbage," insisting that the best way to overcome this fault was to paint directly on the canvas with wide brushes so that the full impact of the paint would impart character and life to a picture.

This revolutionary kind of art teaching, with its emphasis on subjects taken from everyday life, captured the imagination of the students, whose instruction until now had been confined to a repetitious, conservative course of study. Guy Pène du Bois, then a student in the school, said that "life strode into the Life Class," the day Henri arrived to begin his teaching program.

Henri's presence in the city was shared with equal enthusiasm by his associates of Philadelphia days, who had found jobs in New York as illustrators, while awaiting recognition as artists. Choosing the sidewalks of New York as their province, they proceeded to paint the subjects they saw there with a frankness that dismayed the academicians and the Academy would have none of them. Henri's studio again became the rallying place of these young men whose work was considered "revolutionary" in conservative circles.

The men from Philadelphia, Henri, and two more recent additions to the circle, Maurice B. Prendergast and Arthur B. Davies, were ready to prove that they could exhibit independently of the official salon. Plans for an exhibition were discussed, and in 1904 six of them held a collective show at the National Arts Club—Davies, Glackens, Henri, Luks, Prendergast and Sloan. Shinn and Ernest Lawson, who had also joined the group, did not participate.

The effect upon critics and the public was immediate. Charles De Kay wrote in the *New York Times*, for January 20, 1904, "There are six of these gentlemen who are torn to pieces or cracked up as geniuses by their discreditors and friends daily. . . . If the end of the month is reached without duels, the club is in luck." But no challenges were made by either side over the exhibition. The protesting artists were satisfied that the exhibition was the beginning of the long hoped for independent movement.

In 1907, a real break occurred between Robert Henri and the National Academy of Design. Elected to serve on the jury for the Academy's annual exhibition, and a member himself, Henri faced the embarrassment of having his own work questioned by some of the jurors. One of his entries was accepted, the other two were taken conditionally, meaning they might or might not be exhibited at the discretion of the hanging committee. One of Sloan's two contributions was rejected, and the pictures by Luks, Shinn, and Glackens were all refused by the jury. Henri allowed his accepted painting to be shown, but he withdrew the other two. Though he remained a member of the

Academy, he never again contributed to the exhibitions.

The Academy's action at last caused a concerted wave of indignation among the independent artists. Henri, in one of his rare diatribes, stated, "The controversy is not between old and young artists. This action shows that the Academy is hopelessly against what is real and vital in American art. What the outsider must now do is to hold small or group exhibitions so that the public may see what the artists are doing." At meetings held at Henri's studio, a group called The Eight was formed and plans were made for a counter-exhibition, to take place the following year. Henri, Luks, Sloan, Davies, Prendergast, Glackens, Lawson and Shinn, made up the group. The Macbeth Gallery was engaged for the exhibition.

When the show opened on February 3, 1908, the gallery was crowded with interested visitors. Attendance continued excellent throughout the display, and some paintings were sold. Thus ended the first and only exhibition held by The Eight as a group, but the companionship of these men remained as close and spirited as ever.

Meanwhile, Henri had left the New York School of Art to found a school of his own in the Lincoln Arcade, at Broadway and Sixty-fifth Street, where he continued to teach his provocative philosophy of art to an ever-widening circle of students.

In 1910, Robert Henri and John Sloan arranged for another exhibition, larger than the one held by The Eight. This was to be free of jury action and younger artists were to participate. It had a successful run of four weeks and was well attended. The progressive artists were at last being accepted in their own right.

Three years later, the pioneering "Eight" gave their active support to Arthur B. Davies and Walt Kuhn in their brilliant organization of the famous International Exhibition of Modern

Art of 1913, which became known as the Armory Show because of its location in the 69th Regiment Armory, at Lexington Avenue and 25th Street, in New York City.

The Armory Show gave Americans their first full scale view of all that was new in European and American art. Former President Theodore Roosevelt reviewed the exhibition unfavorably for the *Outlook Magazine*. Albert Ryder, old and feeble, came leaning on the arm of a friend, to look at some of his pictures that he hadn't seen in years. Crowds stood before paintings by Cezanne, Picasso, Braque and Duchamp, arguing their respective merits. Robert Henri's long fight for recognition of the "new and vital" in art had finally been achieved.

Although the demands upon his time had steadily increased through teaching and other activities, Henri managed to maintain an active painting program. Tall, lean, with high cheek bones and slanting, piercing eyes, dark haired and possessing a full mustache, Henri went about his work with intelligence and vigor.

His studio overlooking Gramercy Park was always kept in immaculate order for his painting. Brushes and palette stood ready for use at all times, canvases of different sizes were neatly arranged on racks against the walls. In one corner of the room stood a collection of fishing rods for use in his favorite sport, which he pursued with as much enthusiasm as he did his painting.

Henri spent considerable time painting abroad, traveling to France, Spain, Holland and Ireland and choosing subjects for his pictures from among the average people. His manner of painting, which was limited in color at first, gradually developed into a crisp incisive style, sparkling with pure color. The noted critic, Royal Cortissoz, said of Henri's work, "He would fix the model in a good pose, one obviously lifelike, and the rest was a gust of delight in the art of painting . . . he is a realist seeing with his own eyes, and a technician using his own conception of his craft."

Ireland held a particular fascination for Henri. In his later years, he and his wife acquired a summer home in County Mayo called Boycott. He stayed there often during the summer months, painting the Irish folk and fishing the lakes and streams near by for salmon and trout.

Returning to America from one of his trips to Ireland, Henri was taken ill and, after a long sickness, died in New York on July 12, 1929. His work as a teacher of such distinguished artists as George Bellows, Rockwell Kent, Edward Hopper and Gifford Beal had come to an end, but the art spirit he advanced during his lifetime is still having its effect on a new generation of painters.

George Bellows
1882-1925

George Bellows
1882-1925

I N the autumn of 1904, a tall, athletic-looking youth, wearing a rumpled suit, walked with deliberate steps down a railroad station platform in New York. At the age of twenty-two, George Wesley Bellows had arrived in New York from Columbus, Ohio—where he was born on August 12, 1882—to study painting with Robert Henri. Bellows advanced rapidly under Henri's guidance. Within a few years, he was being talked about in progressive art circles as a young man with more than the usual propensity for art.

When he returned home in 1906, for a Christmas visit with his parents, Bellows painted an excellent portrait of his father, who had looked upon his son's preference for an art career with some misgiving. The father's views about the portrait remain undisclosed, but one thing is certain, Bellows's allowance was not increased as a result of it. He was forced to earn extra money for living expenses by playing basketball and baseball in the neighborhood of New York—the two sports in which he had excelled at Ohio State University.

The sprawling city offered an abundant variety of subjects to paint and Bellows, who seemed to follow O. Henry's dictum that ". . . to be an artist . . . you've got to get out into the streets, into the crowds, talk with people, and feel the rush and throb of real life," responded enthusiastically to his new environment.

In the vicinity of the Lincoln Arcade, at Broadway and 65th Street, where Bellows shared a modest studio with friends, stood Tom Sharkey's athletic club, a place where prize fights were held. The young artist visited Sharkey's regularly, to watch the scheduled bouts, studying the movements of the fighters with absorbed interest. The memories of these events were captured by Bellows with force and precision in *Stag at Sharkey's* (Cleveland Museum of Art) and *Both Members of the Club,* (National Gallery, Washington, D.C.) painted in 1909.

Another early impression of New York scenes, called *North River,* was awarded a prize at the National Academy of Design in 1908. On this occasion an official of the Academy wrote to Bellows, saying, "Keep up the good work, my boy. I have my eye on you." At the age of twenty-seven, Bellows was a contributor to all the major art exhibitions, and he had been named an Associate of the National Academy of Design.

In 1910, the artist married Emma Louise Story, of Upper Montclair, New Jersey. They went to live in a house Bellows had acquired, with the aid of his father, at 146 East Nineteenth Street, near Gramercy Park, in New York City. The following year their first daughter, Anne, was born.

Although Bellows' success as an artist was immediate, his financial position was still insecure. Most of the American art collectors were under the spell of the Paris Salon and only a very few of them had the courage to buy progressive American art. This situation led the art critic, Eugene Schuyler, to remark, "They are not patrons of what is native or realistic in painting or sculpture but seem to wish an alliance with the past of other countries. . . . The American painter . . . must either imitate the taint of the museum or set out to become a kind of half-way French or English painter, in order to gain his daily bread."

Rather than compromise his art to this extent, Bellows found jobs teaching art, painting an occasional portrait, doing illustration work, or playing at baseball, to support his family and to continue his own vital kind of painting.

Except for infrequent summers spent outside the city, Bellows preferred working in New York. He had come to know the city well and there was little of it that he had not explored. In the New York described by the writer James Huneker as ". . . this melancholy canyon of marble, steel, and speed," Bellows discovered subjects of poetic charm to paint, such as, *A Day in June,* a view of Central Park, *Gramercy Park* and *Easter Snow,* on Riverside Drive.

In 1913, the artist was made an Academician of the National Academy of Design. He reluctantly retired from active membership in the Academy a few years later, when the institution failed to revive the liberal policies on which it was founded. Meanwhile, he gave what assistance he could to the promotion of the new art movements, playing an active role in the advancement of the Armory Show.

As the critic, Thomas Beer, remarked when this famous exhibition of modern art had ended, leaving in its wake, "overnight a home-grown crop of Picassos and Cezannes . . . George Bellows remained George Bellows." He had never left the country to study art abroad, as others before him had done, and though he viewed with interest the exhibits to be seen in the Armory Show, he preferred to practise his own style of painting, rather than adopt the painting methods used by the foreign exhibitors.

Bellows' method of painting was based upon elements of spirit and execution he had studied in the canvases of the Old Masters at the Metropolitan Museum of Art. He believed, as all intelligent artists have done for centuries, in going to traditional sources for the vision and inspiration he required to establish his own realistic kind of painting.

As an expert also in the graphic arts, Bellows was sometimes engaged to draw illustrations for various publishers. In March, 1915, the year his second daughter Jean was born, Bellows was commissioned by the *Metropolitan Magazine* to make drawings of Billy Sunday's revival services being held in Philadelphia, to illustrate an article on the evangelist. The following year, working mostly from memory, the artist painted *The Sawdust Trail*, a lively impression of Billy Sunday's hour of triumph in the tabernacle, when the "sinners" marched up the "sawdust trail," seeking conversion at the hands of the evangelist.

The outbreak of World War I depressed Bellows. He spent much of his time drawing imaginative sketches of the grim conflict, working this material into his 1918 war series of paintings and lithographs. The painting, *Edith Cavell, 1918*, depicting the heroic British nurse being led to execution by her German captors, is probably the best known picture in this series.

The next seven years were crowded ones for the artist. He devoted himself to the study of J. Hambridge's theory of dynamic symmetry and Hardesty Maratta's system of color, applying both methods to his own work.

At this time also, Bellows painted various members of his family, a stunning romantic series of figure paintings which revealed the use of delicately disposed colors, in contrast to the bold, slashing technique employed in his earlier pictures. These pictures of his mother and Aunt Fanny, of his devoted wife Emma and their two little girls, Anne and Jean, are among the finest figure paintings in American art. A powerful, unconventional interpretation of the Crucifixion was also painted by

Bellows at this time.

The week before his untimely death on January 8, 1925, Bellows spent a happy evening at Robert Henri's studio, in company with his close friend, Eugene Speicher, and other artists. "It seemed later to all of us," Speicher said, "the most fitting spot and happy friendly atmosphere for that sudden and tragic farewell to have taken place."

Index

INDEX

INDEX

ROLAND J. McKINNEY

was educated at Niagara University, the Art School of the Art Institute of Chicago, and abroad.

He has served as director of two of the country's leading art museums, the Baltimore Museum of Art and the Los Angeles County Museum, and was named in 1938 to select and install the American section of paintings for the first Golden Gate International Exposition at San Francisco. Mr. McKinney is presently engaged as Consultant to the Department of American Art, the Metropolitan Museum of Art.

Born at Niagara Falls, New York, Mr. McKinney spent his childhood on the Niagara Frontier, hunting and fishing on the Niagara River, and studying landmarks of this historic region. His principal hobby is collecting paintings, drawings, and prints pertaining to early Niagara.

Mr. McKinney's first book, a monograph on Thomas Eakins, the noted American painter, was published in 1942. He is also the author of books on Degas, the celebrated French artist; *The Eight*, the story of Robert Henri and his circle; and *Famous Old Masters of Painting*.